Portraying Irish Travellers

Portraying Irish Travellers: Histories and Representations

Edited by

Ciara Bhreatnach and Aoife Bhreatnach

Cambridge Scholars Publishing

Portraying Irish Travellers: Histories and Representations,
Edited by Ciara Bhreatnach and Aoife Bhreatnach

This book first published 2006 as hardback. Present binding first published 2006.

Cambridge Scholars Publishing

12 Back Chapman Street, Newcastle upon Tyne, NE6 2XX, UK

British Library Cataloguing in Publication Data
A catalogue record for this book is available from the British Library

Copyright © 2006 by Ciara Bhreatnach and Aoife Bhreatnach and contributors

All rights for this book reserved. No part of this book may be reproduced, stored in a retrieval system, or transmitted, in any form or by any means, electronic, mechanical, photocopying, recording or otherwise, without the prior permission of the copyright owner.

ISBN (10): 1-84718-764-1, ISBN (13): 9781847187642

Dedication

I ndíl chuimhne saothar Nioclás Breatnach agus Tom Walsh, ar dheis Dé go raibh siad.

TABLE OF CONTENTS

Introduction viii
Acknowledgements xiv

Chapter One
Fair Days and Doorsteps: Encounters Between Travellers and Settled People in Twentieth-Century Ireland
Aoife Bhreatnach 1

Chapter Two
Historical Sources Pertaining to Travellers, 1824-1925
Ciara Breathnach 17

Chapter Three
Jack B's Tinkers
Julie Brazil 31

Chapter Four
Privileged Perspectives and Subverted Types:
James Stephens' 'The Demi-Gods'
Paul Delaney 46

Chapter Five
History as Dialogue: An Anthropological Perspective
Sinéad Ní Shúinéar 65

Chapter Six
Navan Travellers Workshops: Tracing the Transformation from Itinerant Settlement to Community Development
Michael McDonagh 86

Chapter Seven
Shelta: Historical and Sociolinguistic Aspects
Alice Binchy 105

Contributors 116

INTRODUCTION

As E.H. Carr pointed out in 1960, a 'mere fact about the past' is not the same as 'a fact of history'. He described how a past event could be retrieved by a historian, whose citation would propose it for 'membership of the select club of historical facts'. Carr further argued that before it could become a full member, it would have to journey from the footnotes to the main text. Of course, many facts about the past are never 'gallantly rescued' by historians or anyone else.[1] Indeed, it took the determined efforts of ideologically committed academics to research and recover the histories of women and marginalised, powerless peoples. The nature of the historical profession is such that the pioneering work of an individual can establish a research area, as the landmark work of E.P. Thompson did for the history of social class. But as Carr points out, one citation by one historian is not sufficient; others must also judge that a 'fact about the past' is also a 'fact of history'. In stark contrast with the numerous books on class that Thompson inspired, David Mayall's historical research on Gypsies has been notable for its lack of successors.[2] Since not all 'facts about the past' are admitted to the formal, professional world of 'facts of history', the dearth of such facts about Irish Travellers is neither unique nor particularly surprising. However, the process of transforming the existence and past lives of Irish Travellers into a 'fact of history' has been slowly and sporadically underway for over ten years.

The landmark volume edited by May McCann, Séamas Ó Síocháin and Joseph Ruane *Irish Travellers: Culture and Ethnicity* (Belfast, 1996) was the first interdisciplinary academic work to analyse Travellers as a distinct group within Irish society. Since then, Bryan Fanning's case study of the historical perception of Travellers in Ennis, County Clare, and Jane Helleiner's exhaustive analysis of Galway City have contributed to a greater awareness of how important the

---

[1] E.H. Carr, *What is History?* (2nd ed., edited by R.W. Davies, London, 1990), p 12.
[2] David Mayall, *Gypsy-Travellers in Nineteenth-Century Society* (Cambridge, 1988), *English Gypsies and State Policies* (Hertfordshire, 1995), *Gypsy Identities 1500-2000: from Moon-Men to the Ethnic Romany* (London, 2003).

historical context is in evaluating Traveller-settled relations.[3] These authors and others, such as Steve Garner, have also used theoretical explanations to understand how and why Travellers were excluded from mainstream Irish society.[4] Many works have examined Traveller-settled relations in the context of racism.[5] Yet historians have been reluctant to engage with work by sociologists and anthropologists on the status accorded to Travellers. It is other disciplines that have been to the fore in presenting Irish Travellers as historical fact. As the title indicates, this volume will deliberately continue the interdisciplinary focus that distinguished previous work on Travellers. Similar to the authors in McCann, Ó Síocháin and Ruane the contributors to this book come from a wide range of disciplines from history, to anthropology to socio-linguistics. Indeed three of the authors here contributed to McCann *et al*'s volume. All the following essays have at their heart a portrayal of Travellers by those on the outside, the majority settled population. Only Michael McDonagh's contribution is from an insider perspective, where an activist, who strives to teach Travellers and settled people alike how to manage cultural difference, explains how representative strategies work on the ground. Yet, what is unspoken in our title is the focus on settled people, called 'country people' by Travellers.

How settled writers imagined Travellers in their texts is examined by Paul Delaney in his chapter on the work of James Stephens. Stephens was one of many Irish writers who drew on a generic Traveller figure that was typically associated with violence, promiscuity, drunkness, theft, poverty, cunning, lawlessness, and loquaciousness. Aspects of this stereotype were present in Stephens' novels *The Demi-Gods* (1914) and *The Crock of Gold* (1912) but the privileged perspective accorded the Traveller characters ensured a complex engagement with the traditional 'tinker' figure. A central argument of Delaney's contribution is that representations of Travellers in the work of settled authors cannot be assumed to be 'inherently reductive and racist' even when the author makes use of unsavoury aspects a 'tinker' stereotype. While Stephens' Travellers are universally and desperately poor, this must be read in the context of his critique of 'prudence and possession', a theme that linked many of his works. Placing the Travellers on the side of the angels in *The Demi-Gods* produced an irreverent novel with a 'serious edge', where a sometimes generic

---

[3] Bryan Fanning, *Racism and Social Change in the Republic of Ireland* (Manchester, 2002), Jane Helleiner, *Irish Travellers: Racism and the Politics of Culture* (Toronto, Buffalo, London, 2000).
[4] Stephen Garner, *Racism in the Irish Experience*, (London, 2004).
[5] Ronit Lentin and Robbie McVeigh (eds), *Racism and Anti-Racism in Ireland* (Belfast, 2002), Ronnie Fay, 'Health and Racism: A Traveller Perspective', in Fintan Farrell and Philip Watt (eds), *Responding to Racism in Ireland* (Dublin, 2001), pp 99-114.

Traveller figure offered a profound critique of capitalism. Genre and authorial intention are never neglected in Delaney's analysis, especially when he draws attention to the ability, however limited, of Stephens to consciously construct the Traveller characters in his texts. Stephens sought to reimagine the Traveller figure but the dangers of engaging with a powerful 'established discursive system' emerge from Delaney's dissection of Stephens' multi-faceted representations. What made Stephens' task difficult was not just his distance from actual, real Travellers but the complexity of the 'discourse on nomadism' that he attempted to undermine.

The wondorous Traveller figure in Stephens' texts is echoed in Julie Brazil's analysis of the occasionally fantastical depictions of nomads in the early work of Jack B Yeats (1871-1957). Yeats drew both English Gypsies and Irish Travellers, but his work is distinct from that of other artists, such as Augustus John, who were also fascinated by nomadic people. Unlike John, Yeats represented Travellers and Gypsies as individual figures, rather than in family groupings surrounded by tents or caravans. The absence of other figures in the most dramatic works cited by Brazil – *A Tinker* and *The Tinker's Curse* (1905) – portrayed the Traveller man as alienated and dislocated from society. The gendered representation of Travellers is a crucial element of Brazil's chapter, as women and men identified by Yeats as 'tinkers' were depicted in starkly different ways. Combining literary studies, the development of the artist and historical context, Brazil has developed a methodology capable of analysing visual representations of a marginalised group. Her innovation is all the more welcome because visual material has not been fully exploited by scholars of Ireland. The potential value of visual sources for those studying the marginal and voiceless is also evident. The neglect of the visual arts in favour of the literary is unsustainable, and Brazil's contribution complements Delaney's analysis of the literary strategies of representation.

Turning to conventional historical sources, the very nature of a document determined how Travellers were recorded and represented as Ciara Breathnach makes clear in her chapter. An awareness of the record-making process is essential for anyone wishing to understand how the history of Travellers can be written. Breathnach outlines the structural considerations that determined how and why information on marginal people was transcribed by those who created the documentary record. Although Travellers might be found in records that detail the lives of the peripatetic people of Ireland, the attention of Poor Law guardians and police were overwhelmingly focused on the individual vagrant rather than the family group. As Breathnach demonstrates, the political concerns with land and possession determined how records were written, largely excluding the landless, and Travellers in particular. However, Breathnach cautions against despair, stressing that a lack of historiography does not signify a complete absence of historical material. Since documentary sources for Irish social history are notoriously patchy, often surviving in abundance in some local areas, Breathnach advocates local history studies to exploit the available resources. The difficulties may seem insuperable, but scholars of women who initially faced similar difficulties have produced outstanding works of history.

To circumvent the inconsistency of official papers on Travellers, Aoife Bhreatnach has turned to alternative source material, chiefly the records of the Irish Folklore Commission and local newspapers. These records have yielded rich results on the texture of Irish social life, details that are rarely preserved in official documents. By analysing the information that settled rural dwellers provided on their relationship with Travellers, a greater understanding of how personal encounters were structured by historical and cultural context emerges. Face-to-face contact on the doorstep was determined by the utililty of goods offered for sale, popular attitudes to alms-giving and by national economic developments. Similarly, the fair day was an occasion whose significance was both intensely local and reflective of general cultural context. The great summer festival of Cahirmee Horse Fair was an occasion for Travellers to demonstrate the enduring success of their material culture. The manner in which one local newspaper portrayed Travellers on a fair day is described in detail here. The consequences for Traveller-settled relations when fairs were undermined by agricultural modernisation, and once welfare superseded charity, are analysed.

The themes of charity and welfare also emerge strongly in Michael McDonagh's contribution on the history of the Navan Traveller Workshop. McDonagh tells how well-intentioned charity dominated the early days of the organisation, when it was called St Jude's Committee for Travellers, but that socially radical Catholic thought transformed the nature of social work in the 1970s and 1980s. Also, attitudes towards Travellers among those concerned with their exclusion from the basic entitlements of society – running water, accommodation – shifted as Travellers themselves became involved in the organisation that was established to help them. McDonagh's own part in this story and the particular history of the Navan committee is frankly told in his chapter, which is as much a history of social work as it is an account of Traveller-settled relations in Navan. The significance of Travellers in developing the welfare agenda in twentieth-century Ireland emerges strongly from his account.

Sinéad Ní Shúinéar's chapter continues the theme of dialogue between Travellers and settled people, but focussing specifically on the nature of communication between a researcher and the research subject. In the course of research, the Traveller informant is being asked by a representative of a powerful, and often hostile, majority for information, which may be vital to the group's protection. As refusal or confrontation would be counterproductive, informants engage in a range of strategies to placate the researcher without compromising their own interests. Ní Shúineár believes that such strategies always operate where the researcher and researched embody a power differential. Her work also addresses how history is understood and negotiated in conversation between Travellers and an academic researcher. Travellers' very concept of history – which aspects of the past are worth remembering, how they are transmitted and their perceived relevance to the present – diverge significantly from standard academic definitions. From a typical researcher perspective, 'essential' issues are deemed irrelevant, and ignored, while 'irrelevant' ones are seen as central. Overcoming her own preconceptions and frustrated expectations in this regard has led her to understand that all history is a cultural construct. The cultural significance of kinship for Travellers emerges from Ní Shúineár's research as the group's most potent expression of how the past that is felt to shape the present. How and why Travellers express Traveller history is clearly a complex process, deserving subtle and sensitive research.

Alice Binchy's chapter also discusses the nature of expression and the role of history. Her analysis of Shelta, the Traveller language, examines how settled observers have commented on its existence. Once again, the problems of differentiating nomads and vagrants in the historical record, emerges. This historical confusion has clearly formed perceptions of Shelta as either a language or an argot. As Binchy points out, linguistic elements alone do not determine how languages are categorised. Yet, in order to better understand the process of language formation, Shelta's lack of an independent grammar structure should be examined. Binchy's thesis that nomadism has formed the very nature of Traveller language demonstrates the importance of movement and mobility in Traveller history.

History runs through all the contributions to this volume, although some historians may still contest its validity as 'real' history. Yet the very diversity of disciplines studying Travellers and their past demonstrates that this group must finally be accorded the status of a 'fact of history'. Strangely, even when Travellers clearly exist as a distinct group in today's society, there continues to be resistance to acknowledging their historical presence. Jim MacLaughlin's book title, *Irish Travellers: Whose Country? Whose History? (Cork, 1995)*, succinctly expressed why this denial of history is politically potent. But, as this volume shows, in literature, art, documents and oral narrative Travellers were recorded. Since their presence was inscribed by members of the majority settled population, it makes recovering their history more difficult, but certainly not impossible. It may primarily be a history of representations and portrayals, but it will illuminate settled and Traveller history alike. That Travellers' understanding of their own history may not accord with a linear, conventional verifiable narrative does not imply that they lack a sense of historical consciousness, or have no history. Echoing Carr, Ní Shúinéar points out that the written history of settled society is also reimagined. All facts of history are fluid, as academic and popular fashions seek new information from historical events. New research is redressing the neglect of Travellers by historians, but other disciplines continue to offer substantial contributions on the relationship between history and Travellers.[6]

---

[6] Aoife Bhreatnach, *Becoming Conspicuous: Irish Travellers, society and the State, 1922-70*, (Dublin, 2006)

ACKNOWLEDGEMENTS

The editors would like to acknowledge the role Dr Bernadette Whelan and Dr John Logan played in bringing this volume into fruition. Some of the essays are based on papers delivered at the Higher Education Authority (HEA) funded 'Sources and representations' symposium hosted by the Department of History, University of Limerick, in May 2005. Two of the contributions – from Aoife Bhreatnach and Sinéad Ní Shúinéar – emerge from research funded by post-doctoral fellowships from the Irish Research Council for the Humanities and Social Sciences. On behalf of our contributors we would also like to express our gratitude to staff at the various institutions, which facilitated research for this work. We would also like to thank Dr Andy Nercessian and Amanda Millar at Cambridge Scholars Press for their assistance. Our colleagues at the history departments of the University of Limerick and the National University of Ireland, Maynooth deserve mention. Finally, we would both like to acknowledge the endless support of our families and friends.

Ciara Breathnach and Aoife Bhreatnach

CHAPTER ONE

FAIR DAYS AND DOORSTEPS:
ENCOUNTERS BETWEEN TRAVELLERS AND
SETTLED PEOPLE IN TWENTIETH-CENTURY
IRELAND

AOIFE BHREATNACH[1]

Some settled people continue to bemoan the demise of a 'traditional' Traveller way of life, where 'tinkers', as tinsmiths, were valued members of rural society, respected for their useful craft skills. The idea of a rural past, free from historical cleavages between settled and nomadic groups is so powerful that local politicians in 1995 wrote that it had vanished only in the previous thirty years.[2] Yet the Commission on Itinerancy in 1963 also described Travellers as victims of economic change that had only recently ended the market for tinware and craft skills.[3] Following the economic modernisation of the 1950s, 'tinker' lost its occupational connotations and the nomadic family in Ireland became a social problem, the 'itinerant'. The belief that Travellers, and their relationships with settled people, were defined by the adult male tinsmith, remains pervasive. An anthropologist, George Gmelch was responsible for bringing the popular belief that Travellers were useful as 'tinkers' but obsolete as 'itinerants' into the formal academic sphere.[4] A formerly harmonious relationship based on the prowess and utility of the tinsmith has provided the historical background to many discussions on the status of Travellers in contemporary Irish society. Yet advocacy groups are to the fore in explaining that the Traveller economy is

---

[1] The author acknowledges the support of an Irish Research Council for the Humanities and Social Sciences Post-Doctoral Fellowship. Thanks to Sinéad Ní Shúinéar for her comments on the first and last draft of this chapter.
[2] *Report of the Task Force on the Travelling Community* (Dublin, 1995), pp 289-90.
[3] *Report of the Commission on Itinerancy* (Dublin, 1963), p. 72, 113.
[4] George Gmelch, *The Irish Tinkers: the Urbanization of an Itinerant People* (2nd ed., Illinois, 1985), pp 42-53.

characterised by flexible self-employment, while Judith Okely effectively demolished Gmelch's argument about occupational obsolescence following shifts in the rural economy.[5] But the past relationship in rural Ireland between Travellers and settled people remains elusive. The characteristics of the historical Traveller economy – tinsmithing, horse-dealing, trading and begging – merit serious analysis, as do the cultural contexts in which the minority encountered the majority settled population. Only by examining the cultural and social mores that governed rural life before World War II can a greater understanding of Traveller-settled relations be reached.

This chapter will examine tinsmithing in relation to other Traveller occupations, particularly focusing on the role of women and children who called to houses selling and begging. How they were received depended on a number of factors, particularly popular religiosity, the extent of subsistence farming, and attitudes to charity and welfare. How and why Travellers were distinguished from other individuals who travelled from house to house seeking alms will be discussed. Moving from the doorstep and country kitchen to a town's main street, the second half of the chapter will analyse the role that fairs, especially the summer festivals of Puck and Cahirmee, played in forming and consolidating Traveller settled relations. The divergent nature of social distance expressed in public and private settings will be explored; the differing status accorded the lone vagrant and the Traveller family will emerge. Since Gmelch rightly expressed a profound official and popular concern with utility, the meaning of exchanges of goods and services in rural Ireland will be addressed.

Encounters with Travellers are described in the records of the Irish Folklore Commission, a source that is used extensively in this chapter. This national folklore collection has been neglected by historians, in contrast to the recently released witness statements in the Bureau of Military History, the contents of which have been scrutinised for insights into political revolution in twentieth-century Ireland.[6] The folklore collection has been ignored not only because Irish historians are wary of non-traditional sources, but because political history continues to dominate the profession. Yet even political events of national importance can be researched in this collection, as Guy Beiner's forthcoming

---

[5] Navan Travellers Heritage Teamwork, *Travellers ... their life and times* (Navan, 1992), p. 6; Judith Okely, *The Traveller-Gypsies* (Cambridge, 1983), p. 50
[6] See for example, Fergus Campbell, *Land and Revolution: Nationalist Politics in the West of Ireland 1891-1921* (Oxford, 2005), Diarmaid Ferriter, *The Transformation of Ireland 1900-2000* (London, 2004).

book on the rebellion of 1798 will demonstrate.[7] The sources for social history are not so abundant that the folklore collection can be ignored, especially since Travellers are but a marginal presence in conventional source material. Two sections of the collection, the Schools Collection from 1937-8 and the Tinker Questionnaire from 1952, contain much significant material, particularly on the economic contacts between Travellers and settled people.[8] As Travellers themselves do not relate their side of the story, the perspective explored here is that of the sedentary, housed population. The mainstays of the Traveller economy were hawking and begging, activities that were the responsibilities of women and children.[9] Opinions of the settled people on begging vary in the sources from hostile to sympathetic, with many expressing no opinion on the practice. Mac Gréine wrote 'they are very persistent, and present such a doleful appearance that the country people usually give them something to get rid of them'.[10] If the proceeds of begging did not suit their requirements, they discarded these immediately 'generally a short distance from the house at which they received them'.[11] This practice would not have endeared them to alms givers, but beggars on foot could not carry large loads. A beggar could hardly refuse any charity offered, even if it did not match his/her needs. The relationship between beggar and alms giver was a complex one and shaped popular opinion of Travellers. Begging and selling could 'torment the housekeepers'[12] and assertive behaviour by Travellers may have challenged perceptions of 'charity cases'.

> The country people never regarded tinkers as objects of charity as they did the poor old beggar-men and women of the old workhouse days. These poor creatures *begged*. The tinkers just *demanded* and God help anyone who left one of them leave the door empty handed. This obtains in the case of the tinkers up to the present day. They wish all kinds of ill-luck to the house and to the crops and to the cattle if they are refused their demands and people are sometimes afraid of their curses.[13]

---

[7] Guy Beiner, *Remembering "The Year of the French": Irish Folk History and Social Memory* (forthcoming, Wisconsin, 2006).
[8] I am grateful to the Head of Department, Department of Irish Folklore, University College Dublin, for permission to reproduce extracts from the Irish Folklore Collection.
[9] Although men manufactured the tinware, they did not sell the goods.
[10] Pádraig Mac Gréine, 'Irish Tinkers or "Travellers": some notes on their manners and customs, and their secret language or "cant"', in *Béaloideas*, iii, no. 2 (1931), p. 172.
[11] Ibid.
[12] [IFC = Irish Folklore Collection Main Manuscript Collection] IFC, 1255, p. 85, UCD.
[13] IFC, 1255, p. 108, UCD.

On the other hand, another respondent to the 1952 questionnaire noted that 'in the very act of begging they set up a feeling of superiority in the minds of those they beg from'.[14] These two excerpts demonstrate contrasting views of the relationship between beggar and alms giver. For Travellers seeking food, clothing or money in order to survive, resorting to curses and petitions was essential and, given their relatively powerless position, understandable. Moreover, that their curses were not taken too seriously is suggested by the saying 'its not worth a tinker's curse'. Prayers and blessings were companions of curses. Nan O'Donoghue knocked on the door of a house with the words '"God save everybody in", saying "I'll say three Hail Mary's for you ma'am if you make us a cup of tea"'.[15] She felt that householders in the West of Ireland wouldn't give to Travellers unless God was mentioned.[16] In Nan Joyce's and Nan O'Donoghue's autobiographies, their dislike of begging is clear. Nan Joyce commented that 'Travellers begging had to make themselves all miserable-looking before they'd be given anything but when you were selling something it was different, you felt better'.[17] But begging was essential in the struggle for survival, as Julia Quinn recalled.

> Then we would start begging off the houses, a grain of flour and anything the woman would give us. A bit of meat, spuds or cabbage, lock of onions, tea or sugar or a bit of butter; we would get a bit in every house. We had to do it, we all begged with the black shawls, the children in our arms, breast-feeding them ... The times were too hard; it was all begging.[18]

Although men made tinware, it was women and children going from house to house who sold the goods. But many Travellers also hawked handicrafts such as artificial flowers.[19] Small items were peddled in rural Cork, 'brooches, hair-grips, tie-pins, beads, laces and pictures'. There was a ready market for these goods among remote rural households. A basket of 'swag' would contain many small items, 'little pictures, hair combs, strainers, scissors, needles, thread, nearly everything you could mention ... shoe laces, polish'.[20] Hawking and begging often occurred simultaneously: once a discussion over selling had concluded, requests could be made for alms.

---

[14] IFC 1255, p. 173, UCD.
[15] Sharon Gmelch, *Nan the Life of an Irish Travelling Woman* (London, 1987), p. 87.
[16] Ibid., p. 130.
[17] Nan Joyce and Anna Farmar, *Traveller an autobiography* (Dublin, 1986), p. 33.
[18] Navan Travellers Heritage Teamwork, *Now and Then* (Navan, 1996), p. 6.
[19] Joyce and Farmar, *Traveller*, p. 31.
[20] Gmelch, *Nan,* p .100.

Yet it would be wrong to examine begging and hawking solely from a perspective of Traveller-settled relations, since non-Traveller men (and occasionally women) also travelled Irish roads, seeking alms and hawking small goods. Distinguishing between peddling and begging could be difficult since, as a prominent politician, James Dillon, pointed out in Dáil Éireann in 1938, selling door-to-door was used to circumvent legislation that outlawed begging. Speaking of his 'old friends', Dillon said that

> ... they circumnavigate the regulations prohibiting their activities by selling studs or bootlaces or something of that kind, so that if a Civic Guard came on the scene you can grab a pair of bootlaces and protest that you were engaged in a commercial transaction; that there was no eleemosynary element in operation at all.[21]

The begging vagrant had long concerned administrators of the poor law, as Ciara Breathnach's contribution to this volume illustrates. Niall Ó Ciosáin has demonstrated that popular attitudes towards begging before the advent of the Poor Law were complex, with categories akin to the deserving and undeserving poor evident in the application of 'boccough' (from the Irish 'bacach' meaning lame) to those pretending to be disfigured or disabled.[22] In spite of persistent government attempts to control vagrancy, a 1925 Garda count proves that 'no fixed abode' included individuals as well as Traveller families.[23] From the Schools Collection gathered by the Irish Folklore Commission in 1937-38, it is clear that Travellers were not alone in using nomadism to maximise subsistence living opportunities. As information was sought under the heading 'an lucht siúil' (literally, the walking people), this source should not be taken as a comprehensive survey of Travellers alone, who were often, though not exclusively, identified as 'na tincéirí' (the tinkers).[24] The interpretation of 'an lucht siúil' as beggars or Travellers varied from school to school but most respondents chose to discuss the vagrant homeless. Children's accounts from late 1930s County Cork are peopled with colourful, often tragicomic local

---

[21] *Dáil Éireann deb.*, lxx, 135 (2 Feb. 1938).
[22] Niall Ó Ciosáin, 'Boccoughs and God's Poor: Deserving and Undeserving Poor in Irish Popular Culture' in Tadhg Foley and Seán Ryder (eds), *Ideology and Ireland in the Nineteenth Century* (Dublin, 1998), pp 93-9.
[23] *Report of the Commission on the Relief of the Sick and Destitute Poor, Including the Insane Poor* (Dublin, 1927), p. 17.
[24] The ambiguous application of labels given to nomads and vagrants is explored by David Mayall, *Gypsy Identities 1500-2000: From Egipcyans and Moon-men to the Ethnic Romany* (London and New York, 2004), pp 54-83 and Leo Lucassen, Wim Willems and Anne-marie Cottaar (eds), *Gypsies and other Itinerant Groups: a socio-historical approach* (London, 1998).

characters 'Paddy Wheel About'[25], 'Dan the fiddler'[26] and 'Jerry the Quality'.[27] In the Schools Collection there were three distinct categories of vagrant: those who sought lodgings; those who sought alms and those who sold items or a skill. These wanderers were separate from and in addition to Travellers.

Male tramps seeking lodgings travelled a regular circuit, staying with the same families for a night at a time, before moving on to the next household on their route. Many were not wholly sane, some were ex-soldiers[28] or former inmates of Industrial Schools.[29] What is striking about these individuals is that although sometimes unconventional and occasionally of questionable sanity, they were written of with considerable affection and sympathy by the school children. They were a part of the local population; their dress, habits and family history were well known. Women were increasingly rare visitors and one woman said 'Travelling women often came around but [now] no women come except gypsy and tinker women'.[30] This mostly male vagrant population was integrated into the local community and though they lived on charity, this was not openly acknowledged.

> These men do not ask for alms. They usually call at dinner time or at tea time. We invite them to join us and they regale us with stories of their adventures while the meal is in progress. They give us news of our friends in Kilkenny, Waterford or Limerick.[31]

Though they did not seek assistance, these men were offered shelter and food. In exchange they told stories, brought news, sang songs or played an instrument.

> The tramps that travel singly look for lodging. They bring news from other places. They generally sleep in an out house or fix a bed for themselves in the kitchen. The people of the house give them their meals.[32]

---

[25] 'Paddy Wheel About' lived in the neighbourhood of Kinsale for 30 years. After his death, local people came to believe that he was Colonel John Hawkes, an ex-soldier who, in the course of his military career, had reputedly led the desecration of a Roman Catholic Church, [IFC S = Irish Folklore Collection Schools Manuscript Collection] IFC S 320, pp 76-78, UCD.

[26] IFC S, 288, p. 325, UCD.

[27] IFC S, 289, p. 261, UCD.

[28] For instance, Johnnie Walker, who lost a hand in battle IFC S, MS 279, p. 65; John Collins, IFC S, 279, p. 230, UCD.

[29] IFC S, 288, p. 327, UCD.

[30] IFC S, 289, p. 259, UCD.

[31] IFC S, 337, p. 92, UCD.

[32] IFC S, 343, p. 33, UCD.

> They often bring news from distant parts. The old people used to gather around them as there was hardly any newspaper at that time.[33]

> They used come round at certain times and bring all the news with them, they were known by 'nicknames' such as 'Straight Road', 'Black Bess', 'Mary from Cork' etc. Some of the men could fiddle beautifully and sing 'come-all-ye' songs.[34]

This was a legitimate currency in a society where entertainment was largely self-made and any diversion from routine gossip welcomed. Séamus Ó Duilearga, who was head of the Irish Folklore Commission established in 1935, pointed to the importance of wandering individuals in the circulation of traditional tales and songs.[35] But a confusion has arisen where descriptions of wandering men and women has been taken to mean Travellers, even though family mobility distinguishes Travellers from those officially labelled as vagrants. A classic illustration of this is in Clodagh Brennan Harvey's work on the English language narrative tradition in Ireland, when she describes Travellers as 'foremost among these nomads' who contributed to the evolution of story-telling in English. The first example Brennan Harvey cites is of a lone adult male, who drew listeners from across the district to the house where he was staying for a period of time.[36] Yet in the second example given, the setting and nature of the encounter were markedly different. A County Clare man spoke of listening to 'a travelling man' who told stories, but tellingly, the man was accompanied by his family. Also, the stories were not recounted in the kitchen of a farmhouse but around the campfire at the side of the road.[37] Some distinction should therefore be made between a single man or woman seeking shelter and a Traveller family, who possessed their own accommodation. Being independent of house-dwellers for shelter, Travellers were accordingly more distant from the family kitchen and fireplace than individuals who sought lodgings. This partly explains why the most memorable portraits of individuals in the Schools Collection were those of homeless men who were familiar figures in a locality, while 'tinkers' were more distant from the respondents.

Popular attitudes to begging and alms-giving emerged particularly strongly from the Schools Collection. A folklore trope categorised as 'Hospitality Blessed', expressed a popular religious culture that praised unstinting generosity offered

---

[33] IFC S, 343, p. 388, UCD.
[34] IFC S, 304, p. 18, UCD.
[35] Cited in Clodagh Brennan Harvey, *Contemporary Irish Traditional Narrative: the English Language Tradition* (Berkeley, 1992), p. 9.
[36] Ibid., p. 10.
[37] Ibid., pp 10-11.

to a nameless, unknown wanderer, who was later revealed to be the Mother of God or Christ himself.[38] Men and women seeking alms worked in this popular Christian tradition, returning charity with prayers and blessings for the giver and his/her family: 'He began his prayers and petitions before reaching the house and continued them for some time after entering the kitchen, in a continuous stream of words'.[39] A beggar would receive alms with blessings such as 'May God spare your health', or 'May God increase your store''.[40] The (long) ending of a petition used by a Mrs O'Donoghue from Macroom was recalled by one informant:

> Ná fhaghad-sa bás go deo go mbéarfaidh mé solas na Nodlag liom! Go saoraidh Dia ó bás i ndorchacht na h-oíche sinn! Go dtugaidh Dia grásta na foidhne daoibh-se is domhsa chun trioblóidí an tsaoghail seo imochar go fulangach foidhneac, agus beannacht Dé le h-anmann na marbh agus le nbhúr n-anam féin ar uair bhúr mbáis![41]

> May you not die at all until I return with the light of Christmas! May God save us from death in the darkness of the night! May God give the grace of patience to you all and to me to carry patiently and passively the troubles of life and God's blessings be with the souls of the dead and your own souls on the hour of your death!

The supernatural consequences for refusing hospitality could be dramatic, as in the folklore category of the 'Greedy Peasant Woman', which told of generosity rewarded and meanness punished.[42] One child recounted a local story in which a beggar woman refused lodgings brought a plague of rats upon a family that ended only when she was granted £10 and lodgings for the rest of her life.[43] When Traveller women cursed or blessed householders, they appealed to a powerful popular tradition that was also inhabited by homeless men and women. Despite the overwhelmingly positive depiction of tramps in this source, not everyone was welcoming; 'some people like to see them coming but others have no welcome for them'.[44] The authorities were not necessarily sympathetic to the plight of vagrants; in 1925, the persistent begging of a 'deaf, dumb imbecile' in Clonakilty County Cork was suppressed by Gardaí.[45]

---

[38] See S. Ó Suilleabháin and R. T. H Christiansen, *The Types of the Irish Folktale* (Helsinki, 1967), number 750, p. 147.
[39] IFC S 326, p. 90, UCD.
[40] IFC S 337, p. 93, UCD.
[41] IFC S 326, p. 31, UCD.
[42] Ó Suilleabháin and Christiansen, *Types of the Irish Folktale*, number 751, p. 147.
[43] IFC S 343, p. 407, UCD.
[44] IFC S 343, p. 33, UCD.
[45] Superintendent M. Troy to Chief Superintendent, 28 Aug. 1925, (NAI DJ H207/4).

Although Irish legislation had outlawed begging since 1542, the spirit of the law had apparently made little impression on popular generosity. Individual alms-giving continued in the mid-twentieth century, although it was believed to be declining in 1938.[46] It seems that reform, rather than prohibition changed attitudes to begging. If the term 'travelling people', as one respondent insisted, was applied only 'to a fast diminishing number of old and infirm people', then benefits for the elderly would have affected their living standards.[47] The state pension, which lifted the elderly out of abject poverty, was twice cited as a reason for the decline in the number of individuals seeking alms.[48] The numbers of Irish elderly availing of the pension after its introduction in 1908 was considerably more than expected and, as Cormac Ó Grada has shown, the payment made a substantial difference to living standards.[49] Mel Cousins has demonstrated that the 1930s saw an increase in the numbers eligible for welfare benefits,[50] even if the payments remained small. Provision for the unemployed was meagre until 1938, when the benefits improved.[51] As state subsistence was seen to improve, tax and rate payers may have felt that individual alms giving was no longer needed. Under these circumstances, tolerance for begging may have declined. More important than government regulation in ending alms was development in the rural economy that can be classified as 'modernisation'. The growth of the rural bus service and motorisation has been blamed for ending the market for Traveller hawkers[52] but the increased monetarisation of the rural economy had other effects also. Until after World War II, potatoes, vegetables, eggs, dairy products and meat were produced in many rural households. When every household produced a small food surplus, there was ample available for Travellers who called to the door. As farmers specialised and concentrated on commercial production, they ceased to produce their own food.[53] Farming households bought food in market towns, replacing farm produce with goods from the grocery shop. There was no longer a potato pit in the back garden, or a

---

[46] IFC S 276, p. 101; IFC S 276, p. 102; IFC S 289, p. 259, UCD.
[47] IFC S 347, p. 443, UCD.
[48] IFC S 347, p. 441; IFC S 276, p. 101, UCD.
[49] Cormac Ó Grada, '"The Greatest Blessing of all": the Old Age Pension in Ireland' *Past and Present*, no. 175, 1 (2002), pp 124-61.
[50] Mel Cousins, *The Birth of Social Welfare in Ireland 1922-1952* (Dublin, 2003), pp 205-7.
[51] Section 4 of the Unemployment Assistance (Ammendment) Act, 1938/2 [Éire] (20 Jan. 1938) increased benefit rates.
[52] Kevin C. Kearns, 'Irish Tinkers: an itinerant population in transition', *Annals of the Association of American Geographers*, 67, 4 (1977), p. 540.
[53] George Gmelch also cited the end of subsistence farming as an important change in the lives of Travellers, Gmelch, *Irish Tinkers,* p. 45.

side of bacon hanging from the rafters to share with men or women seeking aid, which had been formerly dispensed as food. Developments in the rural economy did not affect all areas of the country equally[54] and Travellers may not have been immediately and dramatically worse off. But the extension of the welfare system was closely followed by the end of subsistence farming, and such apparently unrelated changes had a cumulative effect on the position of Travellers.

As the circumstances of Traveller-settled encounters on the doorstep were transformed in the 1940s and 1950s, so too was the interaction between the two groups on the fair day, a central social and economic event. From weekly or monthly markets in towns and villages to the great annual fairs, it was by these gatherings rather than the calendar that the rural community measured time.[55] At such gatherings, people of all classes and origins met and mingled; wealthy farmers and dealers rubbed shoulders with beggars, ballad singers, fiddlers, pedlars, and gamesters. Historically, fairs such as the infamous Donnybrook fair were occasions for lawlessness and bloodshed.[56] A great seasonal gathering of people from near and far was license for a 'moral holiday' which was cathartic and often linked to fertility magic.[57] By the twentieth century, the debauchery observed in earlier centuries had ended but ritualistic elements survived. The anthropologists Arensberg and Kimball observed the 'elaborately conventional'[58] economic aspects of fairs in County Clare that were expressed in the relationship between the small farmer and the cattle dealer. Fair days were significant events in the lives of Irish people, urban and rural, but were especially important for determining attitudes to the minority, nomadic population. The formal records relating to fairs may be limited to charters and tolls but newspaper accounts provide important insights into these gatherings. Such descriptions are particularly important in discerning how Travellers were perceived in a fair setting.

---

[54] In considering change in rural Ireland, regional disparities must not be forgotten. For example, 'By 1975 almost every farmer over 5 acres in Wexford had a tractor while at the other end of the scale less than 25% of farms in Mayo had made the transition', Tim O'Neill, 'Tools and Things: Machinery on Irish Farms', in Alan Gailey and Daithí Ó hÓgáin (eds), *Gold under the Furze: Studies in Folk Tradition Presented to Caoimhín Danachair* (Dublin, 1982), p. 101.
[55] E. Estyn Evans, *Irish Folk Ways* (London, 1989), p. 260.
[56] Ibid., p. 263.
[57] Ibid., p. 256.
[58] Conrad M. Arensberg and Solon T. Kimball, *Family and Community in Ireland* (2nd ed., Cambridge, Mass., 1968), pp 288.

Travellers congregated in large numbers at the edge of the town hosting a fair. One Cork man commented that Travellers 'never fail to make the days more interesting for their presence'.[59] For a number of days, Travellers and settled people traded and drank together in a confined space. Such gatherings demonstrated the enduring success of Traveller's lifestyle as well as the coherence of their material culture. While Travellers attended all fairs, they featured prominently at the famous horse fairs of Ballinasloe, Puck, Cahirmee and Spancil Hill. Horse fairs, which were not as frequent as weekly or monthly cattle fairs, were held in the spring and summer, and often lasted a number of days. These events were what Patrick O'Connor has described as a 'pleasure fair', where entertainment was as important as trading.[60] Also, the prestige attached to the horse gave such annual events an additional *frisson*. The most expensive animal on a farm, Arensberg and Kimball noted that the horse was the 'the special care and interest of the adult man'.[61] While Arensberg and Kimball described the cattle fair as a 'great testing ground for male prowess, skill, and intelligence' their observations could equally apply the specific arena of the horse fair.[62] Since buying and selling horses successfully is a prized skill, and the potential for loss or profit on horseflesh is significant, the great fairs of Cahirmee and Ballinasloe offered men a public forum in which to test their wits. The combination of masculine display, large amounts of money and summer festivities made for a heady combination. By examining one County Cork celebration of the horse, Cahirmee fair, a sense of how Travellers were perceived in a fair-day environment can be appreciated.

Held in the town of Buttevant for two days each July, the Cahirmee fair was a long established summer festival.[63] The large numbers of Travellers who gathered in Buttevant were viewed with ambivalence by settled observers who betrayed their unease by describing an 'invading army'[64] and 'the great nomad army'.[65] As Cahirmee fair approached in 1930, a journalist described the countryside as 'infested with roving bands of humble horse dealers, gipsy vans

---

[59] IFC 1255, p. 89, UCD.
[60] Patrick J. O'Connor, *Fairs and Markets of Ireland: A Cultural Geography* (Newcastle West, 2003), p. 87.
[61] Arensberg and Kimball, *Family and Community in Ireland*, p. 282.
[62] Ibid., p. 289.
[63] See Denis A. Cronin, 'The great horse-fair of Cahirmee County Cork' in Denis A. Cronin, Jim Gilligan and Karina Holton (eds), *Irish Fairs and Markets: studies in local history* (Dublin, 2001), pp. 124-42
[64] *Kerryman* (Cork ed.), 17 Aug. 1935.
[65] *Kerryman* (Cork ed.), 16 Aug. 1930.

and encampments'.⁶⁶ However, their presence also provoked poetic description and nostalgia for times past, which Travellers were seen to embody. In 1955, Cahirmee had 'lost none of its ancient and "old world" glamour for the "travelling people" of Munster' whose 'gaily bedecked caravans' and piebald ponies converged on the town.⁶⁷ The colour and spectacle of Travellers' camps hinted at the gay abandon of an approaching holiday. So important were Travellers to the fair that the centrepiece of Cahirmee from 1949 to 1958 was the caravan parade. This competition for the most colourful, ornate caravan was organised by the fair committee and eagerly contested by Travellers. The parade was part of a carnival that was designed to revive a somewhat flagging fair in 1948, when the festivities and good advertising helped to reverse the decline of previous years.⁶⁸ The 'gay garlanded magnificence, the beribboned horses, the decorated caravans'⁶⁹ offered an irresistible opportunity to newspaper correspondents to romanticise Travellers. Indeed, the parade organisers capitalised upon the resemblance to the gay Gypsy presented by ornate Traveller caravans by renaming the event the 'National Romany Caravan Parade'⁷⁰ in 1955. According to the *Kerryman* reporter, 'gaily attired Romany youths' took part, yet the prizes were not won by foreign Gypsies but by Sheridans from Cork, Rathkeale and Limerick respectively.⁷¹ For observers and the carnival organisers, Traveller material culture dovetailed with literary allusions to exotic Gypsies. Whether there were Romanies at Buttevant was irrelevant – their exotic presence was assured by perceptions of settled people of the appropriate appearance of Gypsies and Travellers. In 1954, the parade was described as bringing 'a breath of the romance of bohemian life' to the town.⁷² A year later, the caravan parade attracted 21 caravans and more than 7,000 spectators. It was an event 'unique and strikingly impressive in all its richness of gay, brilliant, carefree nomadic life'. The *Kerryman* correspondent lauded the parade as 'a presence of the way of life that has kept Cahirmee of the Horses as, perhaps, the last surviving institute of times that are gone but can never be forgotten'. Remarkably, the task of maintaining tradition was laid firmly on the shoulders of 'the travelling folk and the horse-dealing people of Munster'.⁷³

---

⁶⁶ *Cork Examiner,* 14 July 1930.
⁶⁷ *Kerryman* (Cork ed.), 9 July 1955.
⁶⁸ *Kerryman* (Cork ed.), 3 July and 17 July 1948.
⁶⁹ *Kerryman* (Cork ed.), 8 July 1950.
⁷⁰ *Kerryman* (Cork ed.), 9 July 1955.
⁷¹ *Kerryman* (Cork ed.), 26 July 1953.
⁷² *Kerryman* (Cork ed.), 10 July 1954.
⁷³ *Kerryman* (Cork ed.), 23 July 1955.

While Travellers were exoticised in descriptions of Cahirmee, it must be noted that the fair itself was praised in a hyperbolic manner. The *Kerryman* wrote of Cahirmee: 'It was a word that brought a breath of romance to the workaday world in which we lived. Entwined in every letter of it was an atmosphere that gave forth the exotic scents of the Orient, and the clink of Russian spurs and the rattle of French sabres'.[74] The glorious past when Cahirmee drew buyers from across Europe was often invoked in newspaper reports. Such was the success of caravan parade that the organising committee for County Kerry's Puck Fair imitated the Cork tourist attraction in 1955.[75] The unique nature of Cahirmee's caravan parade was justly celebrated in the local newspaper, because even Appleby fair in Cumbria, a great English horse fair that was inextricably associated with Gypsies, did not place an official celebration of nomad material culture at its heart.[76] That the parade in 1955 was organised by Muintir na Tíre, a self-help organisation dedicated to improving local areas, and the Gaelic Athletic Association, an organisation that championed sporting nationalism, makes it all the more remarkable.[77] These two bodies were representative of the nationalist bourgeois Ireland that MacLaughlin has claimed excluded and stigmatised Travellers, yet in the context of Cahirmee fair, such groups promoted Traveller material culture as distinctive and glamorous.[78] The parade was evidently popular, and became a centrepiece of the rejuvenated, post-war fair.

The allusions to exotic, oriental Romanies dominated newspaper coverage of Travellers at Cahirmee in July, but romance did not entirely obscure Traveller's Irishness, which was alluded to in references to red-haired tinkers. The 'ginger-headed travelling men' and 'the red women of the clans' who congregated at Cahirmee were observed a month later at Puck Fair in Killorglan; the 'red heads of the tinkers' appear to have been intimately associated with summer fairs.[79] In popular tradition, those with red hair were believed to have fiery, ungovernable tempers and Travellers' behaviour at fairs apparently confirmed this belief. Travellers were known for fighting on a fair day, but this did not worry settled

---

[74] *Kerryman* (Cork ed.), 11 July 1953.
[75] *Kerryman,* (Kerry ed.), 6 Aug. 1955.
[76] For more see the Gypsy Collections at the University of Liverpool, (*http://sca.lib.liv.ac.uk/collections/gypsy/appleby.htm*) (13 Apr. 2006).
[77] *Kerryman* (Cork ed.), 23 July 1955.
[78] Jim MacLaughlin, 'The political geography of anti-Traveller racism in Ireland: the politics of exclusion and the geography of closure' *Political Geography* xvii, no. 4 (1998), pp 442-3.
[79] *Kerryman* (Cork ed.), 9 July 1960; *Kerryman* (Cork ed.), 15 July 1961; *Kerryman,* 13 Aug. 1960.

people, who did not participate. A respondent to the Irish Folklore Commission's 1952 questionnaire wrote that 'The tinkers' free fights was a particular feature of the fair and one of the most spectacular.'[80] It was a keenly watched 'blood sport' for those who did not take part.[81] The readiness with which fights were apparently forgotten was noted by settled people, who used the phrase 'like the tinkers' of people who quarrelled frequently but remained friends.[82] Of course, Travellers were not the only people who fought at fairs; O'Connor noted 'Routinely too, fair day had a court sequel.'[83] On a fair day, fights were as much part of the occasion as a carefully organised and staged caravan parade. The spectacle provided by wild, exotic nomads was a central part of the great summer horse fair. Spectacle permitted admiration but maintained distance; it acknowledged difference while containing it as harmless entertainment.

For Travellers, the summer fairs were social and economic highlights of their calendar. Families that were thinly scattered across the country might only meet at such occasions while lucrative trading, dealing and begging opportunities were manifold at a great fair. Yet observers had little interest in what these gatherings meant to Travellers, preferring to describe the pageant of colour and carefree abandon that their appearance presented. Within the fair setting Travellers were rendered picturesque by settled people. Spectacular occasions such as fairs and fights gave ample opportunity for observation but little for participation. It is significant that even at a communal event where people were gathered in great numbers in one place, social distance was carefully maintained. The contact between settled people and Travellers was confined to limited occasions and, even then, was superficial. The conclusions drawn from these encounters were determined by settled values that were not static, as was the case in attitudes towards street violence. Michael Houlihan said of Traveller fights at Puck, 'Before opinions changed it was something of a sideshow at the fair, which drew, rather than scattered crowds.'[84] Unfortunately, it is not clear when this shift in opinion happened. Male prowess in Traveller society was often demonstrated in fights that were designed for internal and external consumption. Internally, the free fight was an obvious substitute for a state legal system that was largely inaccessible to illiterate and nomadic people. Externally, such fights demonstrated the ferocity of a group who were politically and socially marginal. The object could have been to warn settled people from

---

[80] IFC 1255, p. 141, UCD.
[81] John Healy, *The Death of an Irish Town* (Cork, 1968), p. 19.
[82] IFC S 351, p. 208, UCD.
[83] O'Connor, *Fairs and markets*, p. 129.
[84] Micheal Houlihan, *Puck Fair: History and Traditions* (Limerick, 1999), p. 52.

interfering with Travellers – an effect that was achieved, as John Healy's observation that 'spectators' retreated watching 'in fascination and fear', illustrates.[85] Trading was another aspect of masculinity displayed at the fair, where Traveller men were acknowledged experts in horseflesh. This expertise brought prestige in the world of horses, where the ability to judge horses was a talent few could claim to possess. The role of the 'tangler', who helped to secure a deal between buyer and seller, was often adopted by Travellers. In the traditional methods of reaching a deal, Travellers earned 'luck money' and acted as mediators between settled people whose interests were antagonistic in a commercial arena. Tanglers were part of fair convention, giving Traveller men an opportunity to play a role in a formal ritual central to the commercial gathering.[86]

Yet the fairs that were the lifeblood of Irish rural life suffered a significant blow after World War II when agricultural life changed dramatically. Horses were replaced by tractors so appreciation of Traveller equine knowledge was diminished. Cattle and sheep marts were constructed on the edge of towns, making traditional street fairs redundant. These developments took place suddenly 'without anybody realising what a difference it would make'.[87] Even as Cahirmee was refashioned as a pleasure fair with a 'carnival' organised to attract visitors, livestock fairs across Ireland began to decline. Yet Travellers continued to adhere to an obsolete calendar of fairs, visiting towns because of old associations. Nioclás Breatnach recalled Travellers from Tipperary visiting Dungarvan in County Waterford even after the horse fair that had originally drawn them had been discontinued.[88] The decline in these regular, formulaic often ritualistic gatherings, ended a social forum where Travellers and settled people gathered together in large numbers. The fairs had provided an important opportunity for Travellers to display their knowledge of horses, as well as flaunt their material culture or wealth. In a fair milieu, Travellers were accorded a certain respect and role, with Cahirmee's caravan parade an example of overt celebration. Once fairs ceased to occupy a central economic and social role in

---

[85] Healy, *The Death of an Irish Town*, p. 19.

[86] A Traveller man was described as a 'tangler from Rathkeale', Kerryman (Cork ed.) 8 July 1950. For more on the role of tanglers see Arensberg and Kimball, *Family and Community in Ireland*, p. 291 and Patrick Logan, *Fair Day: the story of Irish fairs and markets* (Belfast, 1986), pp 98-100.

[87] Logan, *Fair Day*, p. 101.

[88] Interview with Nioclás Breatnach, Glanmire, County Cork (29 Dec. 2001). Breatnach worked for the Irish Folklore Commission as a full-time collector in the Ring Gaeltacht, County Waterford, see Nioclás Breatnach, *Ar Bóthar Dom* (Rinn Ó gCuanach, 1998), p. 40.

Irish life, encounters between Travellers and settled people were more limited. But Travellers continued to visit market towns, visits that became an intrusive nuisance without the structural justification of a fair.

The two contexts for Traveller-settled relations examined here – the doorstep and the fair – altered after World War II. Yet it would be a mistake to see a stark contrast between harmonious relations in the 1930s and strained interactions in the 1950s, for Travellers had always been set apart from house-dwellers. The distinction between individual homeless men and Travellers has been almost wilfully misunderstood by observers anxious to portray an idealised rural society free from social distinctions. But Travellers were never social intimates of house dwellers in the way wandering individuals who slept by the fire sometimes were. Long before attitudes to charity and alms-giving began to shift, opportunities for personal contact between Travellers and settled people were restricted. But the loss of the fair day was, in the long term, more serious for Traveller-settled relations because of the complexity of the interactions at such gatherings. Once the fair setting was eliminated, Traveller-settled relations were increasingly confined to the doorstep, where begging became an oddity as welfare support grew. Individual contacts made through begging were on a notably less equal footing than encounters in the context of horse dealing. Seeking alms placed Travellers in a certain position, where pleading rather than dealing characterised their encounters with the housed population. As subsistence farming also declined, tolerance for begging faded. More or less simultaneously, tinsmithing lost its economic value but this development alone cannot explain the transformation of Traveller-settled relations. If fairs had endured even after tinkering had ended, begging may not have come to characterise the Traveller-settled encounter. Once opportunities for the two groups to meet were confined to the doorstep, perceptions of Travellers shifted, and became increasingly determined by a belief in their inevitable poverty and deprivation. The social distance between the two groups that separate accommodation allowed subsequently became an unbridgeable gulf between the caravan and the kitchen.

CHAPTER TWO

HISTORICAL SOURCES PERTAINING TO TRAVELLERS, 1824-1925

CIARA BREATHNACH[1]

The purpose of this chapter is to account for some of the primary sources that are useful for historical research on Irish Travellers. It focuses particularly on the period from the 1824 Vagrancy Act to 1925, when An Garda Síochána (the Irish Police force) conducted the first count of Irish homeless.[2] This chapter also outlines some of the problems associated with researching a marginalized, uncategorized group that did not adhere to the dictates of administration under British or independent Irish rule.[3]

For the historian, locating Irish Travellers in official Irish sources during this era can be a very difficult process, indeed, the first major consideration must be nomenclature and how it changed over time.[4] Travellers are usually referred to in occupational terms like, tinker, peddler or hawker, and, like many other landless people, they do not feature in the primary nineteenth-century Irish historical sources, for instance, the Tithe Applotment, the Ordnance Survey

---

[1] I would like to thank Aoife Bhreatnach for reading and rereading this chapter!
[2] Saorstát Éireann, *Report of the Commission on the relief of the sick and destitute poor including the insane poor* (Dublin, 1927), p. 17. Vagrancy Act, 1824, 5 Geo. 4, c.83.
[3] Recently the subaltern Irish historiography has expanded somewhat. Recent studies include: Fintan Lane and Dónal Ó Drisceóil (eds.), *Politics and the Irish working class, 1830-1945* (Palgrave, 2005).
[4] This work deals exclusively with Irish sources but the wider availability of records in digital format deserve mention, notably the Old Bailey project:
http://www.oldbaileyonline.org/. For an account of the project see Tim Hitchcock, 'A new history from below', *History Workshop Journal*, 57, (2004), pp 294 - 298. British Parliamentary Papers are also available free of charge on few websites such as http://www.eppi.ac.uk/ and http://www.bopcris.ac.uk/.

memoirs or the Griffith's Valuation.[5] In addition the various trade directories exclude references to nomads. Census forms allowed for only four categories of housing and temporary dwellings were not included. Unsurprisingly, Travellers are omitted from the census, since the basis for enumeration was the household, but this limitation was exacerbated by the fact that enumerators took liberties. To give an elementary example, women and their contribution to family-run business were seriously under-represented because individual enumerators categorised them as unwaged housewives.[6] Despite the absence of statistical evidence and the fact that scholars are at odds about the 'Traveller origin' theories, we can take as standard that there was a notable nomadic population active within Ireland during this timeframe. Literary sources, such as, the work of Synge, Lady Gregory, W.B. Yeats and James Stephens, visual sources, the artwork of Jack B. Yeats and anecdotal accounts, for example, those presented in evidence to government appointed commissions, all attest to the existence of travelling tinkers, landless labourers, beggars and gypsies.[7] An interesting point to note is that these sources along with memoirs, such as, Hugh Dorian's mid-nineteenth century work from Ulster, make little distinction between the different types of nomad. Dorian notes 'the newcomers or yearly visitors consisted of tinkers, pedlars, pipers, show-men and beggars, and many otherwise idle with no profession'.[8]

Another fact that we can also assume is that, with the exception of fairground people and the duration of fairs and markets, Travellers predominantly occupied rural rather than urban spaces.[9] This comes into line

---

[5] Tithe Applotments of Ireland were carried out in each civil parish between 1823 and 1838 to ascertain how much landholders should pay towards the upkeep of the Church of Ireland. They are listed by townland and householder. For an account of the Ordnance Survey memoirs see Gillian Doherty, *The Irish Ordnance Survey, history, culture and memory* (Dublin, 2004), p. 49. Doherty argues that 'In these reports there was little consideration of the harsh reality of poverty'. Griffith's Valuation was a survey of property ownership in Ireland. It was carried out between 1848 and 1864, its purpose was to ascertain how much each landholder could afford to contribute in rates to support the administration of the new Poor Law Unions.
[6] E. Roberts, *Women's work, 1840-1940* (Cambridge, 1988), pp 8-9. See also Whelan, B., (ed.) *Women and paid work in Ireland, 1500-1930* (Dublin, 2000).
[7] Jane Helleiner, *Irish Travellers: Racism and the Politics of Culture* (University of Toronto Press 2001), pp 33-39. Paul Delaney, 'Representations of Travellers in the 1880s and 1900s', *Irish Studies Review*, 1 (2001), pp 53-68. See also Julie Brazil's contribution to this volume.
[8] Breandán Mac Suibhne and David Dickson, (eds.), *The outer edge of Ulster: a memoir of social life in nineteenth-century Donegal* (Dublin, 2000), pp 212-3.
[9] Travellers sometimes 'wintered' in urban tenements but this was a temporary arrangement.

with the findings of the 1909 Poor Law Commission that noted how most of the general population was unwaged and was primarily engaged in agricultural occupations or 'in service to cultivators'.[10] In 1923 the Drew Commission reported that agriculture still accounted for '75 per cent of the total wealth production of An Saorstát' (Irish Freestate).[11] Travellers provided a range of services to the cultivator and they enjoyed a symbiotic relationship until such services became obsolete with modernization, and the later mechanization, of farming practices.[12] That Travellers occupied the rural rather than the urban precludes their official documentation because throughout the nineteenth century urban-based Royal Irish Constabulary (RIC) officers were regularly used to conduct enumerations and reports. Sedentary attitudes to nomads in the rural setting differed greatly to treatment and perceptions of them in the urban. Crowther notes in Victorian Britain that in urban areas the function of police officers was to 'identify habitual or "professional tramps"', who were seen as the 'main threat to social order'.[13] The perspective of officials, such as, medical officers and occasional inspectors, combined with the limitations of their specific remit and different degrees of diligence and awareness is a key aspect of why our now more neatly classified, 'Travelling Community' is hard to find. For the most part of the nineteenth century government dealt with rural Ireland in a two dimensional fashion distinguishing between the landed and the landless poor. This is exemplified in land legislation that responded to agrarian discontent, which further segregated and perpetuated the phenomenon of landed and landless by seeking a prohibitively expensive security for land purchase.[14] The Royal Commission on Congestion Ireland (RCCI) recommended that labourers should be prevented from buying land under the 1909 Land Act on the grounds that it merely stalled the prospect of emigration for one generation.[15] Most legislation dealing with rural Ireland in the late nineteenth and early

---

[10] *Royal Commission on the Poor Laws and Relief of Distress* [HC, 1909] Cd.4630, xxxviii

[11] Saorstát Éireann, *Reports of the Commission on Agriculture* (1927), p. 75 NLI, R/25.

[12] For further information see G. Gmelch, *The Irish Tinkers: the Urbanization of an Itinerant People* (2nd ed., Illinois, 1985).

[13] M. A. Crowther, 'The Tramp', in R. Porter (ed.), *Myths of the English* (Cambridge, 1992), p. 91

[14] For further information see P. Bull, *Land, politics and nationalism* (Dublin, 1996); B.L., Solow, 'A new look at the Irish land question', *Economic and Social Review*, 12 (1981), 301-14; B.L., Solow, *The Irish land question and the Irish economy, 1870-1903* (Boston, 1971).

[15] RCCI, Final Report, [HC 1908], Cd. 4097, xlii. p. 787. See also F. H.A. Aalen, 'The rehousing of rural labourers in Ireland under the labourers (Ireland) Acts 1893-1919', *Journal of Historical Geography,* 12 (1986), 287-306. M. Fraser, *John Bull's other homes: state housing and British policy in Ireland, 1883-1922* (Liverpool, 1996).

twentieth century concerned the acquisition of land or property, neither of which was of interest to the Traveller.

Distinctions between the Traveller and the general poor are difficult to detect and while it is not accurate to socially rank the Travellers below the lowest class of landless, with respect to nineteenth and early twentieth century primary records, it is convenient. Economically Travellers as a group have never been homogenous and by the mid-twentieth century it comprised various social strata.[16] Social ranking in Traveller society was inextricably linked to occupation and income, some of the higher ranks included metal workers, cattle jobbers, horse and antique dealers, while the lower echelons relied on dubious sources of income such as peddling, fortune-telling and begging. Unfortunately, the social and economic composition of Traveller society is not borne out in official nineteenth century sources. For all intents and purposes Travellers can be categorised as 'landless' but it is important to note that during the nineteenth century there was another class of partially-sedentary but partially-nomadic, landless labourers who were not Travellers. They were probably akin to what Arthur Young noted during his late eighteenth century tour, a 'wandering family' living in temporary dwellings crudely constructed using readily available materials such as sticks, furze and ferns. He described them as a landless people who earned a living 'how they can, by work, begging and stealing; if the neighbourhood wants hands, or takes no notice of them, the hovel grows into a cabin'.[17] Part of the annual cycle for the landless was to take to the roads either to seek casual labour, to beg, or both. But a possible distinction[18] between the landless labourer class and the Traveller is that the former was more likely to maintain a connection to a fixed abode to which they returned at stages of the year.[19] An 1835 report noted another sect of what was is described as 'strange beggars' that could be 'seen in crowds of a fair-day'.[20] Begging was a traditional female Traveller occupation but this reference is not exclusive to

---

[16] The social hierarchy of Irish Travellers is clearly seen in the *Report of the Commission on Itinerancy* (Dublin, 1963), pp 78-83. The statistics are based on censuses compiled by an Garda Síochána in 1944, 1952, 1956, 1960 and 1961.

[17] Arthur Young, *Arthur Young's Tour in Ireland, 1776-1779* (edited and with introduction by Arthur Wollaston Hutton, London 1892), p. 40.

[18] This does not imply that Travellers had no connection to a fixed abode it is possible that they had, however, this requires further research.

[19] N. Ó Cíosáin, 'Boccoughs and God's poor: deserving and undeserving poor in Irish popular culture', in T. Foley and S Ryder (eds.) *Ideology and Ireland in the nineteenth century* (Dublin, 1998), p. 95.

[20] *First report from His Majesty's Commissioners for inquiring into the condition of the poorer classes in Ireland,* [HC, 1835], xxxii

them, there were large numbers of rural people who were highly mobile and also relied on alms as a livelihood.

Notwithstanding social, political and economic circumstances and agrarian unrest in the nineteenth century, from a very early stage the idle but able-bodied poor were identified as a societal menace, while those who were homeless were of even more concern. The historic treatment of vagrants under penal and poor law codes had been very harsh.[21] Various aspects of homelessness, or, rooflessness were officially classified as indictable offences in 1824 (under the vagrancy act) and some clauses remained until 1997.[22] The 1824 act was not as severe as the preceding sixteenth-century laws but it outlawed various practices and occupations associated with the Traveller tradition, for example, fortune-telling, palmistry and begging. It also made sleeping rough, squatting in derelict buildings, sleeping in a tent or wagon, indictable offences.[23] Yet most entries of identifiable Irish nomads in annual British Parliamentary reports imply references to the classic solitary 'tramp' rather than members of a community. For example, Irish county magistrates and jails were obliged to account for the type and number of crimes committed on a county basis and returns are given for persons charged with the vagrancy offence.[24] A general overview of the 1839 report shows that per county, numbers committed on the charge of vagrancy was low, testimony to the fact that the law was not enforced rigidly, rather it was used selectively. In the case of Armagh jail only two were committed on the charge, one was acquitted by jury's verdict and the other was deemed insane; genders were unspecified. Sentences were rarely passed down and offenders were released on the condition that they found 'security for good conduct'.[25] Even during the famine when returns should have escalated the number of persons committed did not rise too much. In the hard-hit areas of

---

[21] David Dickson, 'In search of the old Irish Poor Law' in R. Mitchinson and P. Roebuck, (eds.), *Economy and society in Scotland and Ireland, 1500-1939* (Edinburgh, 1988), pp 149-159.
[22] Under section 28 of the 1988 Housing (Ireland) Act the 1824 Vagrancy Act was amended by the deletion of 'every person being found in or upon any dwelling house, warehouse, coach-house, stable, or outhouse, or in any enclosed yard, garden or area, for any unlawful purpose'. Further amendments were made under the Criminal Justice (Public Order, Ireland) Act 1994, section 12 and under the 1998 Housing (Ireland) Act.
[23] For further information on poor law in Ireland see Law Reform Commission, *Report on Vagrancy and Related offences* (1985), pp 1-18. See also M. Cousins, *The birth of social welfare in Ireland, 1922-1952* (Dublin, 2003), pp 10-13.
[24] *Return from clerks of Counties in Ireland of number of persons committed for trial, 1839*, [HC, 1840] xxxviii
[25] *Return from Clerks of Counties in Ireland of Number of Persons committed for Trial, 1839*, [HC, 1840] xxxviii

Donegal numbers were low in 1847 but this may be a reflection of the impact the newly established workhouses had on absorbing swelling masses of evictees and homeless poor.[26] Galway noted only one vagrancy charge in 1845 and 298 in 1847 and 242 in 1848. In this case it was alleged that local magistrates were 'playing the system' and ridding their respective districts of paupers by sending them to county jails.[27] Statistically the vagrancy problem escalated following the famine, as Caitriona Clear shows in her study of judicial records and jail registers, the numbers tried for the offence increased steadily between 1866 and 1914.[28] However these vagrancy charges usually effected individual tramps not Travellers, who had some form of an abode and family members to give good account of them. In contrast with the 'idle able-bodied' solitary figure, Clear notes that in popular opinion, 'complete families of Travelling traders or craftsmen were never perceived as a public order problem' because they were supporting a family, they were skilled and so had ways of earning a living.[29]

The nineteenth-century rural economy was barely fluid and when alms were not forthcoming it was customary for beggars to avail of official poor relief from time to time. Poor relief had traditionally been borne by local benevolence, but following the extension of the Poor Law to Ireland in 1838 it became systematic and the onus of providing for the poor rested with the union.[30] It was financed by a rate collected by guardians at union level; landlords owning or tenants renting over four acres paid a poor rate and those whose holdings were over one but under four acres paid a lower rate, called a 'county cess'.[31] People were overtly opposed to paying for poor relief: McDowell notes how the payment of the poor rate was 'violently resisted in some unions', and that collectors had to be accompanied by police or military personnel.[32] Although it was initially abhorred by reticent ratepayers, it was recourse for the frugal and relieved the guilt associated with begrudging alms to the poor. Under this regime the poor

---

[26] *Return from clerks of counties in Ireland of number of persons committed for trial, 1847*, [HC, 1848] lvii
[27] *Select Committee on Poor Laws (Ireland), Eighth Report*, Minutes of evidence, [HC, 1849] XV Pt.I.559.
[28] Caitriona Clear, 'Homelessness, crime, punishment and poor relief in Galway 1850-1914: an introduction', *Journal of the Galway Historical and Archaeological Society*, 50, (1998), pp 118-34.
[29] Ibid., p. 126.
[30] V. Crossman, *Local government in nineteenth-century Ireland* (1994). R. B. McDowell *Irish public opinion, 1750-1800* (Westport, 1975).
[31] R. O Shaughnessy, 'Local Taxation in Ireland', in J.W. Probyn, (ed.), *Local Government in the United Kingdom* (London, 1882), pp 319-383.
[32] R. B. McDowell *The Irish administration, 1801-1914* (London, 1964), p. 177.

were divided into 'deserving' and 'undeserving' categories, that is those who were not responsible for their misery (the widow, the orphan, the blind, the aged) and those who could be held accountable, such as, the rogue, the vagabond, or the single homeless vagrant.[33] As responsibility for the poor came to be borne by all, it became a major contributory factor in the negative sedentary opinion towards them and more specifically towards transient or nomadic poor, who were not likely to repay the system. Ó Cíosáin argues, using a combination of socio-linguistic and official sources, that unsympathetic treatment of the poor was nothing new and the evidence is embedded in the etymology of certain Irish words, such as, *maide croise* and *bacach* .[34] He highlights with evidence from the 1835 Poor Law Commission that the Catholic hierarchy played an active part in exposing fraudsters and undeserving poor.[35]

The poor law itself was mainly administered 'indoors' and is more popularly referred to as the workhouse system. In essence it was designed to deter potential beneficiaries. Under the workhouse system males, females and children were separated and dietary standards were deliberately designed to be lower than that of a landless labourer.[36] A prerequisite for entering the workhouse was to give up all worldly possessions; this included signing away land holdings thus placing all inmates on a level pegging. Given the harsh weather conditions, the resulting poor harvests and the dependency Travellers had on the agrarian economy, it is likely that some 'wintered' in the poor house but this is not discernable without a systematic analysis to identify surnames and entries of possible Traveller trades. Some indoor registers are extant and they contain a wealth of untapped material but have yet to be examined by scholars interested in writing the social history of the poor.[37] Each register has an index of surnames at the beginning and gives an entry number which details, gender, age, marital status, whether deserted or orphaned child, profession, religion, disability, name of spouse, number of children, observations of the pauper's condition on admission, electoral division or townland in which resident, date of

---

[33] Robert Jutte, *Poverty and deviance in early modern Europe* (Cambridge, 1994), p.8
[34] *Maide croise* meaning crutches but is literally translated as cross sticks, *bacach* means beggar but literally translates as lame
[35] N. Ó Cíosáin, 'Boccoughs and God's poor', p. 99.
[36] C. Kineally, 'Administration of poor law in Mayo, 1838-1898', 6, *Cathair na Mart,* (1986). See also H. Burke, *The people and the poor law in nineteenth-century Ireland* (Dublin, 1987). Mel Cousins, *Social welfare law* (2nd ed. Dublin, 2002),
[37] The National Archives of Ireland (NAI) hold indoor registers for the Balrothery Union (part of County Dublin), Bawnboy Union (part of County Cavan), Dromore West Union (part of County Sligo) and Lismore Union (part of County Waterford). Indoor registers also survive for 19 other unions and are held at various County Archives.

admission and date of discharge or death in workhouse.[38] These entries could be cross-referenced with Traveller surnames, occupations and their associated geographical circuit.[39] The workhouses were regularly used for short-term relief, for example, Thomas Joyce, a South County Dublin tailor, entered the workhouse, where his wife was already in 'the sheds', on 19 February 1848 and was discharged on 28 February 1848.[40] Technically it was easy for nomads to float in and out of the workhouse, Henry Meredith's overnight stay in Bandon workhouse, in 1920, provides a classic example. Meredith (46) admitted himself, his wife Sarah (42) and their children Joseph (10) and Mary (7) on 31 July and they were discharged on 1 August. Meredith was described by the workhouse master, Timothy Forde, as a dealer who 'frequents fairs and markets with his family'.[41] In addition to the indoor registers some workhouse Masters' Journals survive, the entries are sporadic but contain interesting observations of inmates.[42] There is no doubt that the poor were well able to manipulate the system and when the poor law extended to incorporate outdoor relief schemes in 1848, Travellers probably did avail of employment opportunities in public works. Details of schemes can be found in annual reports to parliament, but they are statistical and do not include personal details for employees.[43] However, some local archives hold additional, but miscellaneous, Poor Law material and these have yet to receive due consideration with the profile of the poor (as opposed to the institution) in mind.[44]

Finding references to quintessential Traveller trades in Roman Catholic Parish records can also be a productive exercise and random entries of 'tinker' can be found under 'occupation'.[45] It is worth noting that it is not accurate to categorise all tin or metal workers as Travellers, nor was tinsmithing the only occupation

---

[38] NAI, BG 74 G4 South County Dublin, PLU register DF admission and discharge book 4, 23 November 1847 to 16 August 1848.
[39] *Report of the Commission*, p. 151. See also Ní Shúinéar in this volume.
[40] NAI, BG 74 G4 , p. 97.
[41] Cork City and County Archives (CCCA) BG/42/G1, p. 15. Bandon Union indoor register,.
[42] CCCA, BG/42/F1, Bandon Union Master's Journal, 1921-1925, p. 23.
[43] *Return of number of persons receiving outdoor relief in unions in Ireland, February and March 1848*, [HC, 1848] 309, liii.
[44] Extant indoor registers can also be found at Cork City and County Archives, Donegal County Archives. For a complete listing of county archives (and in some cases their holdings) see http://www.nationalarchives.ie/links/IRLarchives.htm.
[45] Nenagh Civil Marriage records, register 7, p.17, entry 2. I am grateful to Nora O' Meara for this reference. While Travellers were predominantly Catholic, the records of other denominations such as Church of Ireland vestry records could also be fruitful.

pursued by them. Travellers must have engaged in casual agricultural labour but this is particularly hard to substantiate as there was a wage-related social hierarchy at play. For example, the farm servant was, as Breen defines, a waged labourer that lived in their master's homes. These jobs were privileged and their procurement, in many respects, hinged largely on social connections.[46] Fitzpatrick's study of full-time farm labourers highlights that the need for such a class was in serious decline at the close of the nineteenth century and this facilitated the rise in casual harvest work.[47] Boyle cites a late nineteenth century *Lyceum* article that noticed how 'of the unskilled agricultural labourer in Ireland … comparatively little is heard', but even less has been written about Traveller involvement.[48] Statistical data to prove that Travellers engaged in agricultural labour is lacking (payment was usually in kind and is therefore difficult to trace) but there are many anecdotal accounts showing that this tradition was long-established and continued well into the twentieth century.[49] A proper exploration of the records of the Irish Folklore Commission, oral history sources as well as early Irish television footage would provide further information on the extent to which Travellers engaged in agricultural labour and how their acceptance of payment in kind benefited the farming community.[50]

Regardless of the symbiotic relationship that existed between Traveller and the country people, rural Ireland was becoming increasingly class conscious from the late nineteenth century, with small farmers being quick to differentiate between themselves and cottiers, while cottiers disassociated themselves from landless and so on.[51] Lane, citing Micheal J.F. McCarty's early twentieth-century work, argues that in Munster 'intermarriage between small farmers and

---

[46] R. Breen, 'Farm servanthood in Ireland, 1900-40', *Economic History Review,* 36 (1983), pp 87-102.
[47] D. Fitzpatrick,'The disappearance of the Irish agricultural labourer, 1841-1914', *Irish Economic and Social History,* 7 (1980), pp 66-92.
[48] John W Boyle, 'A marginal figure: the Irish rural labourer' , in S. Clark and J.S. Donnelly jr., *Irish peasants: violence and political unrest, 1780-1914* (University of Wisconsin Press, 1983), pp 311-338.
[49] Carles Salazar, *A sentimental economy: commodity and community in rural Ireland* (Providence, RI, 1996), p. 42. *Report of the Commission on Itinerancy*, p. 72.
[50] The nature of IFC records are discussed in Aoife Bhreatnach's contribution to this volume. Oral History projects are emerging all over Ireland, in conjunction with History and Folklore Departments at the various Universities, local libraries and History Societies. The Radio Telefís Éireann (Irish National Television company) Archive is deserving of thorough examination, as does the Irish Film Archive in Temple Bar, Dublin, which also has an abundance of untapped material.
[51] For further information see D. S. Jones, Graziers, *Land reform and conflict in Ireland* (Washington, 1995).

labourers is rare, and, when it occurs, is deemed a "downfall" for the small farmer's family', Lane notes that in Ulster 'intermarriage between farmers and labourers was similarily frowned upon'.[52] This trend of social stratification intensified as the twentieth century progressed. Indeed it was encouraged by the state, for example, under the labourer's housing acts efforts were made to improve living conditions. Although labourers' cottages were built to relatively high standards, such identifiable public housing compounded their position in the social hierarchy; below those who described themselves as farmers.[53] While this issue warrants further analysis, these acts catered primarily for landless agricultural labourers and it is likely that many who benefited from it were previously, of the partially-nomadic calibre that is, those who traveled in search of work.[54] The provisions of the labourer's housing acts, particularly the 1906 act, provided opportunities for upward mobility and subsequently the lines between this partially-nomadic class and the Travellers became more clearly defined. In contrast with Travellers, the former class was always an aspiring sedentary people.

From a historical perspective for the period 1910-1920 (with the exception of the war years) we rely largely on literary works and visual material for representations of a Travelling people. This was a time of modernisation and of considerable political, social and cultural upheaval. Politically, the issues of Home Rule, war and rebellion dominated this era; socially, cultural nationalism had made a profound impact on Irish society and in many respects this encouraged a redefinition of Irish identity that was entrenched in sectarian terminology.[55] In this climate the differences between the Travellers and the sedentary classes became more pronounced. Despite the enormous contribution the Anglo-Irish literary revivalists played in acknowledging the significance of Traveller culture, in fictional works both W.B.Yeats and Lady Gregory promulgated a poor image by using 'tinkers as their agents of destruction'.[56]

---

[52] M.J.F. McCarthy, *Irish land and Irish liberty* (London, 1911), p.121, cited in, Fintan Lane, 'Rural labourers, social change and politics in late nineteenth-century Ireland', in F. Lane and D. Ó Drisceóil, (eds.), *Politics and the Irish working class,* p. 116. For an account of the social status of labourers in the twentieth century see Dan Bradley, *Farm labourers: Irish struggle, 1900-1976* (Belfast, 1988), pp. 19-20.
[53] *Reports from the Poor Law Inspectors on labourers' dwellings* [1873, C.764], xxii
[54] Crossman, *Local government*, p. 52. Crossman argues that guardians in Munster and Leinster availed more of the labourer's housing legislation than Ulster, where it was noted in 1885 that there was no need to build such accommodation
[55] A. Jackson, *Home Rule, an Irish history, 1800-2000* (London, 2003)
[56] Cornelius Weygandt, *Irish Plays and Playwrights* (Boston, 1913), p. 53. A. Price, *J.M. Synge, collected works, vol II,* (Washington, 1982), p. 202-4. Maurice Bourgeois, *John Millington Synge and the Irish Theatre* (London, 1913), p. 72. Contemporary critics

With the foundation of Saorstát Éireann and the ensuing civil war the gulf between the sedentary and the nomad widened further.[57] Secret languages, such as the Traveller Cant, were viewed with suspicion and in times of political and social upheaval Travellers 'were often victimised as "outsiders" and "spies" by colonial settlers and the settled Irish alike'.[58] Unfortunately, the resulting acrimonious relationship between the Traveller and the sedentary spells good fortune for the researcher. Early Dáil records, newspaper articles and petty sessions all consider the interactions between both groups.[59]

Administratively, the diversity of the Irish lower classes began to be recognised in 1906 when a Royal Commission recommended that the 'existing system of keeping many different classes in the same workhouse should be abolished'.[60] But this epiphany did not extend to examining the plight of varying degrees of nomadic people. For the poor some advances were made with the establishment of a social welfare state most notably with the passing of the Old Age Pension Act, 1908 and the gradual implementation of sickness and unemployment benefits. The old mechanisms of poor law administration were gradually dismantled between 1916 and 1925, a number of workhouses were closed and some were burned during the civil war. When the civil war ended the fledgling government could focus on serious issues like poverty, and it adopted a similar

---

noticed how Synge's work was questionable because he derived information 'from wholly untrustworthy guides –tramps, tinkers, ballad-singers and other vagrants who, like the proverbial Irish jarveys, are apt to misinform the inquisitive visitor'.

[57] Breda Gray, *Women and the Irish Diaspora* (London, 2004), p. 62-3.

[58] Jim Mac Laughlin, 'The political geography of anti-Traveller racism in Ireland: the politics of exclusion and the geography of closure', *Political Geography,* (1998), p. 421. Peter M. Hart, *The I.R.A. and Its Enemies: Violence and Community in Cork, 1916-1923* (Oxford, 1999), p. 303. Indeed during the civil war nomads were viewed in a more pronounced state of distrust, Peter Hart estimates that along with Protestants and ex-soldiers, tinkers and tramps comprised 14% of informants. Hart's figures are very questionable and it is unfortunate that he lumps tinkers with tramps but is interesting to note how the various social pariahs –for social economic and cultural reasons- have been categorised together

[59] Some Petty Sessions records are held at the NAI. See also http://historical-debates.oireachtas.ie.

[60] *Viceregal Commission on Poor Law Reform in Ireland* [1906, Cd.3202], li. Minutes of evidence, 1906 Cd. 3203, li, 441; Cd. 3204, lii. The purpose of the 1906 Commission was to 'Generally to inquire and report whether any, and what administrative and financial changes are desirable in order to secure a more economical system for the relief of the sick … and all classes of destitute poor in Ireland, without impairing efficiency of administration'. It concluded that the workhouse system was not suitable for Ireland, which had a healthy 'able-bodied' population that was willing to work but unable to find gainful employment.

approach to the British of appointing a commission to assess problems and make recommendations. One such commission and resulting report was the *Commission on the relief of the sick and destitute poor including the insane poor*. It was published in 1927, and it was marginally more inclusive in its distinction between the various poverty-stricken classes then resident in Ireland. Essentially, the purpose of this inquiry was to help devise a modern 'poor law'; it was mainly concerned with the sick and destitute poor and was adamant that the expenditure on 'healthy persons and the incorrigibly idle' be avoided.[61] While the terms of reference purported to be 'very comprehensive' and it aspired to finding 'social problems lying almost on the fringe of the poor law' it reverted to the draconian delineations of deserving and undeserving poor outlined in 1824.[62] However, a striking feature of this ambitious report is the inclusion of a census of homeless persons conducted by An Garda Síochána at the bequest of the commission. This census was of 'homeless persons observed wandering on the public highways' on a November night in 1925. It found a total of 339 adults homeless in the Metropolitan area and 2066 adults and children homeless outside the metropolitan area.

	Outside Metropolitan area			Metropolitan area		
	Men	Women	children	Men	Women	Children
Travelling in search of work	248	33	44	116	18	
Willing to undertake casual labour but unfit or unwilling to work continuously	238	48	58	120	18	
Habitual tramps	652	416	614	34	7	
Old and infirm persons	150	63	14	13	5	
Bona-fide pedlars, hawkers, etc	141	77	122	7	1	
Total	1,429	637	852	290	49	

Given the significant gains landless labourers had made under the housing acts the data breakdown implies that Travellers were counted in this census. Travellers moved in a family unit and the fact that children are not included in the metropolitan count confirms that they were still predominantly rural based. On the other hand, at that time of the year Traveller families could have been

---

[61] Saorstát Éireann, *Report of the Commission on the relief of the sick*, p. A2
[62] Saorstát Éireann, *Report of the Commission on the relief of the sick*, p. B

'wintering' in tenements and therefore not 'seen wandering'. Even though the methodology was highly flawed and the remit was narrowly defined (homeless, persons in the Metropolitan area, those outside, and those seen wandering) it is the first official record that refers to homelessness as a social condition that effected entire families by noting 'homeless persons and their dependent women and children'.[63] The overall report was primarily concerned with the sick poor, the insane, and the destitute poor, and Travellers were not a priority. The primary result of this report was that the remaining work houses were turned into county homes and outdoor relief was renamed home assistance.[64] No provisions were made for homeless people and their care was left to the voluntary sector and organisations such as the Society of St Vincent de Paul.[65]

On the surface it is easier to outline where Travellers were omitted from official nineteenth century sources than it is to find official references to their existence. The fact that such a distinctive class was largely ignored by nineteenth-century enumerators stems from a homogenous attitude to the rural Irish in general. Administrators made few exceptions and did not acknowledge the diversity of the Irish social fabric and little changed with the emergence of independent Ireland.[66] However, as E.P. Thompson espoused in the 1960s the 'scanty evidence' argument is not convincing enough.[67] We cannot assume that the existing historiography is a true reflection of the records and sources need be revisited and reinterpreted. Like Travellers, women at all levels of Irish society are poorly and inadequately represented in historic sources, yet in the past thirty years gender historians have produced excellent work by engaging imaginatively with limited material.[68] Future researchers should take example

---

[63] Saorstát Éireann, *Report of the Commission on the relief of the sick*, p. 17
[64] S. Ó Cinnéide, *A law for the poor: a study of home assistance in Ireland* (Dublin, 1970)
[65] *Bulletin of the Society of St. Vincent de Paul, Supplement for Irish Conferences*, vol.LXVI, (1921), p. 3 The Dublin night shelter of the St Vincent de Paul was opened in 1915, by 1920 it was dealing with 16,786 admissions and provided nearly 27,000 meals annually.
[66] *Report of the Commission on Itinerancy*, 1963. It was not until 1963 that the first Government report recognising Travellers was published, and then they were referred to as an 'itinerant problem'
[67] E.P. Thompson, *The making of the English working class* (London, 1968), p. 233.
[68] Maria Luddy and Cliona Murphy (eds) *Women surviving: studies in Irish women's history in the 19th and 20th centuries* (Dublin, 1990). For more recent studies see Whelan (ed), *Women and paid work in Ireland*. Rosemary Raughter (ed.) *Religious Women and Their History: Breaking the Silence* (Dublin, 2005). Maria Luddy, 'Moral rescue and unmarried mothers in Ireland in the 1920s', in *Women's Studies: An Interdisciplinary Journal*, 30: 6 (2001), pp 797-817. Lindsey Earner-Byrne, *Mother and*

from this work and approach Irish Traveller history with the same level of creativity.

Child: Maternity and Child Welfare in Ireland, 1920s-1960s (forthcoming, Manchester University Press).

CHAPTER THREE

JACK B'S TINKERS

JULIE BRAZIL

Identifying the Irish Travellers or 'tinkers' as a distinct grouping from the ordinary rural poor at the close of the nineteenth and early twentieth century is a very difficult task. This is due to the lack of formal records as some scholars have outlined.[1] The nature of the Traveller's nomadic life, which has resulted in this scarcity of written history, has led anthropologist Sinéad Ní Shúinéar to examine their oral tradition.[2] The early recording of Travellers has depended on the intellectual endeavours of the settled community, notable examples being the playwrights of the Anglo-Irish Literary Revival at the turn of the twentieth century.[3] Both Paul Delaney and Mary Burke have respectively examined the representation of Irish Travellers in the drama and literature of the literary revival.[4] Given the fragmented and disparate sources available for the study of Travellers and their place in Irish society, the visual record must not be neglected. The valuable use of paintings as a source in Irish historiography is gradually being acknowledged[5] but images of the Irish Travellers have been

---

[1] See Aoife Bhreatnach, 'Travellers and the print media: words and Irish identity' in *Irish Studies Review*, 6, 3 (1998), p.285 and Jim MacLaughlin, *Travellers and Ireland: Whose country, whose history?* (Cork, 1995).
[2] Sinéad Ní Shúinéar, 'Irish Travellers, ethnicity and the origins question' in May McCann, Séamas Ó' Síocháin and Joseph Ruane (ed.), *Irish Travellers: culture and ethnicity* (Belfast, 1994), pp 54-77.
[3] For example John Millington Synge and his play, *The Tinker's Wedding* (1907) and Douglas Hyde's, *An Tincéar agus an tSidheóg* (1902).
[4] See Paul Delaney, 'Representations of the Travellers in the 1880s and 1900s' in *Irish Studies Review*, ix, no.1, (2001) and Mary Burke, 'Eighteenth-century European scholarship and nineteenth-century Irish literature: Synge's *Tinker Wedding* and the orientalizing of Irish Gypsies' in Betsey Taylor FitzSimon and James H. Murphy (ed.) *The Irish Revival reappraised* (Dublin, 2004).
[5] Fintan Cullen, *Visual politics: the representation of Ireland 1750-1930* (Cork, 1997) and Brian O' Kennedy and Raymond Gillespie (ed.), *Ireland: art into history* (Dublin, 1994).

relatively ignored. This article will examine the visual representation of the Irish Travellers in the early work of Jack B. Yeats (1871-1957).

Yeats is a well-known Irish painter, more renowned for his later oils, but he was also an accomplished illustrator and writer.[6] He was a very prolific artist and he created in his lifetime nearly 2,000 oils and around 700 watercolours during the years 1897 to 1955.[7] His paintings and prints of the Irish Travellers amount to a small but significant portion of this work and therefore warrant a more in-depth study.[8] In all he created twenty four works (from 1900 to 1928) that can be identified as a 'Traveller' or nomadic theme but this work focuses on two watercolours, a print, two oils and some sketchbook drawings representing the Travellers from 1905 to 1922. One of the most notable features of Yeats images of the Irish Travellers is that they are gendered and provide individual studies of the male and female Traveller; he rarely portrayed the community group.[9]

Yeats showed a consistent but moreover early interest in nomadic minority groups and this fascination began in England with the Gypsies. By 1897 Yeats was painting watercolours of Gypsies at horse races and markets. In the late nineteenth century, Irish Travellers frequently travelled and stayed for periods of time in England, Scotland and Wales.[10] But Yeats did not identify, in his work, Irish 'tinkers' at the races and fairs, which he attended in Devon. The difference in Yeats' later portrayal of the Irish Travellers in contrast to the English Gypsies is most significant in dress and physical appearance. Yeats tended to paint the Gypsy skin in a dark tone that highlighted their ethnic origins.[11] In contrast, the Irish Traveller in his work usually has red hair, pale skin and their dress is not very different from the rural Irish peasant.

---

[6] For a comprehensive biography on Yeats' life and work see Bruce Arnold, *Jack Yeats* (London, 1998). Hilary Pyle has catalogued Yeats' entire work in various publications including *Jack B. Yeats: his watercolours, drawings and pastels* (Dublin, 1993) and *The different worlds of Jack B. Yeats: his cartoons and illustrations* (Dublin, 1994).

[7] T.G Rosenthal, *The art of Jack B. Yeats* (2nd ed., London, 2003), p.51.

[8] See Julie Brazil, *The representation of the Irish Travellers in the paintings and prints of Jack B. Yeats, 1900-1928* (M.A thesis, 2005, University of Limerick). Also Tricia Cusack, 'Migrant Travellers and touristic idylls: the paintings of Jack B. Yeats and post-colonial identities' in *Art history*, xxi, no.2 (June, 1998), pp 201-216.

[9] Only later, in the oil painting *Tinker's Encampment the Blood of Abel* (1942) did Yeats portray a Traveller camp in a thick impasto style. The symbolic image of this painting comments on the terror of war.

[10] Artelia Court, *Puck of the droms: the lives and literature of the Irish tinkers* (London, 1985), p. 17.

[11] The first written account of the Gypsy in England was in 1505 and they were described as being physically different with darker skin, eyes and hair. It was in the late eighteenth

Yeats was born in London in 1871, his parents John B. Yeats (1839-1922) and Susan Pollexfen (1841-1900) had six children all together. Both families were of Anglo-Irish descent, the Yeats' were from landed gentry and the Pollexfens emanated from the merchant class in Sligo.[12] John and Susan Yeats' marriage was a difficult one as John B. Yeats, who was initially trained as a barrister, became an artist. In brief, he was not successful in his lifetime. Because of their precarious finances the Yeats family lived between Dublin and London over a period of twenty-three years. Susan Yeats returned home frequently to Sligo along with her children to receive help from her parents.[13] As a result of this financial insecurity she suffered from depression and so it was decided that Yeats, the youngest, would stay with his grandparents in Sligo, spending his formative years there from nine to sixteen, living a relatively privileged upbringing in rural but, Anglo-Irish, Ireland. In 1887, Yeats returned to live with his family who were then residing in London, and there he began his formal artistic education. He attended four art schools between 1887 and 1889; the training focused on drawing from both life models and antique statues. During his art education, Yeats made a concerted effort to find paid work and specifically targeted magazines that were fashionable in late nineteenth-century London. Subsequently he spent ten years working as a journalistic illustrator for publications like *Ariel, Chums, Lika Joko* and *Punch*. He also worked for the sporting paper *Paddock Life,* which required him to attend race meetings, football and rugby matches, trotting races and hunts all over the British Isles. He enjoyed working for this paper, even though it was physically demanding, and stayed for two and half years.[14] The illustrations he produced for these papers were usually of a comic tone, (for example, he caricatured people) however, they were also based on observation and fieldwork.

After ten years as an illustrator Yeats married in 1897 and moved to Devon to concentrate on becoming a professional artist. He was fascinated by the local life of west Devon, the farmers, local children, sailors by the docks and the English Gypsies and he began to record these people in a large sketchbook. This was to be the first sketchbook of approximately two hundred and by 1900 he was using them everyday to record everything and everyone around him.[15] As

---

century when the link was made between the Gypsies in Europe and their origins that began in India. Burke, 'Eighteenth-century European scholarship and nineteenth century Irish literature', pp.205-6.

[12] R.F Foster, *W.B. Yeats: the apprentice mage* (Oxford, 1997), pp 1-5

[13] Grifford Lewis, *The Yeats sisters and the Cuala* (Dublin, 1994), pp. 9-10.

[14] Pyle, *The different worlds of Jack B. Yeats*, pp 18-19.

[15] A collection of over two hundred sketchbooks from 1898 to the 1940s is housed in the Yeats archive in the National Gallery of Ireland.

time progressed the sketchbooks became smaller and they fitted neatly into his pocket, which meant that Yeats could sketch people unnoticed at public events like fairs and markets. In one such sketchbook dated from 1903, he captured images of Gypsies and their involvement at the horse races in Devon. In the drawings he made notes of their attire, physical expressions and interactions with other people at the race. He returned to the studio with the sketchbooks and created many watercolours including *The Gypsy Jockey* (1903). English artists, like Augustus John (1878-1961) who created artwork for the *Journal of the Gypsy Lore Society,* were painting Gypsies exclusively in their own environment; for example, they concentrated on their caravans and exotic clothing.[16] In Yeats' approach, he chose to take a closer look at the interaction of Gypsies with the sedentary population and in paintings like *The Gypsy Jockey* this interest was connected to their strong association with horses.

In 1905 John Millington Synge (1871-1909) was commissioned by the Manchester Guardian to travel around the west of Ireland and to write about the people living in the poorest areas and their daily hardships. The editor of the paper suggested that Yeats accompany Synge as an illustrator. According to Bruce Arnold, Yeats' biographer, they were more like 'kindred spirits' rather than friends, as they did not spend a lot of time together before or after the trip but he points out they shared similar views of Ireland and its people.[17] Coming from a similar Protestant middle-class background, they both admired the people of the road and the freedom of their lifestyles and, according to Pyle, both men found a deep interest in the 'tragedies and grinding existences' of the rural men and women of Ireland.[18] The shared sympathy which both Synge and Yeats felt towards the peasants of the west resulted in their work focusing on people before custom and folklore.[19]

---

[16] Augustus John was president of the Gypsy Lore Society from 1937 to 1961. He was a portrait painter and painted W.B. Yeats in 1912. He adopted a nomadic lifestyle and contributed songs, vocabularies and drawings of the Gypsies, which he met in England and abroad. He met Coppersmith Gypsies in Marseilles in 1910 and he created a series of drawings which were later published in the *Journal of the Gypsy Lore Society* vol.5 1911-12, 'Calderai Gypsies from the Caucasus'.
[17] Arnold, *Jack Yeats*, p.133.
[18] Hilary Pyle, 'Many ferries: Jack B. Yeats and J.M Synge' in *Eire-Ireland,* xviii (1983), p.18.
[19] Pyle, 'Many Ferries', p.19. Synge's *Aran Island,* an objective comment on the people of the island, disappointed Lady Gregory, who wanted him to focus more on the islanders' folk beliefs and superstitions.

In previous years to the commission for the *Manchester Guardian,* Synge had walked all over Wicklow collecting and recording stories and taking photographs of the rural peasants and the people of the road, making an effort to collect material at the races and fairs.[20] Harold Orel suggests that Synge, like his contemporaries, did not distinguish between tinkers and Gypsies and other travellers.[21] Synge uses the term 'vagrant' very liberally in his writing and in most cases he is referring to the individual tramp (a separate entity from the Travelling community). Synge admired the 'scholarly' tramp and from his writings he found the 'wanderer as outcast ... by choice and temperament as much as by circumstances: "the gifted son", either of middle-class or peasantry'.[22]

Figure.1 *A Tinker* (1905) – See Centrefold

During their one-month expedition, which unlike other travellers was mainly done on foot, Synge and Yeats collected stories and images about the traditional work of the west including kelp-gathering and burning, traditional thatching and observed the road works set up by the Congested District Board.[23] Both men carried notebooks, recording wherever they went.[24] The incidents that Yeats came across on the trip as well as the many characters he observed, inspired later paintings; *A Tinker* (1905) was probably one of them.[25] According to Pyle, *A Tinker* (Figure. 1) is one of the artist's finest studies of human character.[26] Even though Pyle does not elaborate on this opinion of the painting, it is a distinctly different portrait from others he produced during this period. The wandering man of the road, successfully captured in this three-quarter-length portrait, appears to be walking in the west of Ireland (indicated by the low stonewalls that are in the fore and middle ground in the painting). *A Tinker* is noticeably different from another Yeats' watercolour *The Man from Aranmore* (1905) in terms of character and presence. The man in the latter painting stands proudly and confidently in front of a quayside, well dressed in the native costume of the Aran Islands. The colours in this work are soft and muted. In contrast, Yeats used black ink in *A Tinker* to draw the heavy outlines of the figure and to create the darker tones within the painting, while his use of salmon

---

[20] Nicholas Greene (ed.), *Interpreting Synge* (Dublin, 2000), p. 28.
[21] Harold Orel, 'Synge's concept of the tramp' in *Eire-Ireland,* vii (1972), p. 55.
[22] Ann Saddlemeyer, 'The essays as literature and literary source' in George Gmelch and Ann Saddlemeyer (eds.), *In Wicklow, West Kerry and Connemara* (Dublin, 1980), p. 20.
[23] James Hack Tuke (1819-1896) and others conducted their travels by jaunting car.
[24] Pyle, 'Many Ferries, p. 23.
[25] Ibid., p. 30.
[26] Pyle, *Watercolour, drawings and pastels*, p. 141.

pink shades in the evening sky created a sinister atmosphere. The most interesting feature of this painting is of the Traveller's face, which is sharp and made distinctive with his long, narrow nose. The overall impression of the Irish Traveller in this painting is not a sympathetic one; it is portraying a figure that does not belong in any particular place, even in the barren area he is captured in.

In stark contrast to Pyle's later judgement an unknown critic with the *Irish Times* in 1905 reacted hostilely saying that *A Tinker* was 'a distinct caricature of an indispensable factor in country life. The face and figure are grotesque, and we utterly decline to believe that such accurately typifies any numerous Irish class'.[27] Indeed the west of Ireland was not devoid of class awareness in the late nineteenth century as small holders viewed their position as higher than landless labourers and no doubt the wandering poor.[28] Marilyn Gaddis Rose considers that when Yeats painted the Irish peasant he 'was accurate and respectful, disposing the peasant as subject so that the viewer, also, will be encouraged to regard the subject with respect. His farmers ... are not, like jockeys and tinkers, larger-than-life, they are people'.[29] Yeats was less inclined to treat the Irish Travellers, as he had done the Irish peasants, in a formal and accurate representation using the skills of his early career as a journalist illustrator. Instead, in *A Tinker* Yeats successfully portrayed a 'marginal' person in society with the use of caricature. The art critic and historian Ernest Gombrich, claims that the tradition of the caricaturist, in nineteenth-century Europe, played and distorted with the likeness of his subject and this distortion invariably expressed how he felt about his 'fellow man'.[30] Yeats used this stereotypical image in many other works he produced of the male Traveller. In general the image was a negative one with the face of the male tinker appearing pinched and almost mean. According to Stuart Hall the use of stereotyping in the representation of the 'other' was essentially the exercise of a 'symbolic power' in society and tended to occur where 'there are gross inequalities of power'.[31] Similarly, in the middle of the nineteenth century the Irish peasant was caricatured harshly in

---

[27] *The Irish Times*, (cutting, 1905) (NGI, Yeats archive, Box Y Mus Par 25A, 1891-1925).
[28] Ciara Breathnach, *The Congested Districts Board, 1891-1923* (Dublin, 2005), p. 44.
[29] Marilyn Gaddis Rose, 'Jack B. Yeats' picture of the peasant' in Daniel J. Casey and Robert E. Rhodes (ed.), *Views of the Irish peasantry, 1800-1916* (Hamden, 1977), p. 194.
[30] E.H Gombrich, *The story of art* (16th ed., London, 1995), p. 564.
[31] Stuart Hall, 'The spectacle of the "other"' in Stuart Hall (ed.), *Representation: cultural representations and signifying practices* (London, 1997), p. 258.

publications like *Punch* and *Lika Joko* where the simian and brutish features of the 'Paddy' were circulated throughout middle-class, Victorian England.[32]

A Tinker reflected the negative image of the 'fierce' Traveller male and conveyed the message that he was a threat to the rural settled community. Jane Helleiner, who has conducted research on the historic and contemporary stereotypes of the male and female Traveller in post-independent Ireland, claims that in the Irish Free State a strong anti-Traveller feeling developed in the local newspapers and in government debates. She argues that this led to the conclusion that the Irish Traveller male was a direct threat to the isolated rural housewife.[33] Even though *A Tinker* was painted seventeen years prior to the formation of the Irish Free State, it alludes to the roots of anti-Traveller feelings that Helleiner has documented.

Figure. 2 *The Tinker's Curse* (1905).
© Estate of Jack B. Yeats/ DACS 2006

---

[32] See Lewis P.Curtis, *Apes and angels: the Irishman in Victorian caricature* (Devon, 1971).
[33] Jane Helleiner, 'Women of the itinerant class: gender and anti-Traveller racism in Ireland' in *Women's Studies International Forum*, xx (1997), p. 277.

In the watercolour *The Tinker's Curse,* (1905), a Traveller man is wildly throwing his arms around in a rage down a house-lined street.[34] The setting is possibly in a village in the west of Ireland where the superstition of the 'tinker's curse' was prevalent.[35] It was described by one critic 'as the most powerful picture in the exhibition, the most powerful presentation of life.'[36] *The Tinker's Curse* stood out as a strong painting to the critics with its unique choice for subject matter: 'the face of wild, open mouthed imprecation, the shaggy hair, the wretched garments, and the fury of the running figure, represent something that hundreds of our citizens would have no knowledge of but for the pencil of Mr. Yeats'.[37] Therefore, this painting has a voyeuristic element to it as it gives the viewer an opportunity to witness up close a tinker in a spasm of rage uttering his curse.

Paul Delaney refers to the 'tinker's curse' that changed the personality of the Traveller from 'taciturn and silent' into a person who was to be feared and it was used in a play to transform the character of a Traveller into a more threatening one.[38] He argues that the curse was the symbol of the 'dirtiness' of the Traveller, which was compounded by his use of vulgar language. The 'tinker's curse' was used in plays to indicate the 'outsider' position that the Traveller held in the play and this curse was thought to be a reflection of their persona in general. Yeats' representation of the Traveller in *The Tinker's Curse* is of a person on the fringe of society, symbolized by the absence of other people in the painting, similar to *A Tinker*. In the latter work the Traveller looks out at the viewer, however, in *The Tinker's Curse* the Traveller directs the curse away from the viewer's gaze yet it does not show the intended victim. Similar to *A Tinker* the absence of people in this painting enforces the visual impression of an alienated person in society; there is no doubt that the figure is a pariah. Yeats was familiar with how wary the rural people were towards the Travellers as he indicated in a letter to his patron John Quinn. In the letter Yeats recalled a friend's 'wild notion of going through Ireland with a pack this year, he thought of going as a tinker but I put him off that idea, because in Ireland the country people don't like tinkers, they think there's something not right about them'.[39]

---

[34] A colour reproduction of *The Tinker's Curse* was not located but a black and white image is reproduced in Padraic Colum, *My Irish year* (London, 1912), p. 92.
[35] *The Freeman,* (NGI, Yeats archive, Box Y Mus 25A, 1891-1925).
[36] *Sinn Fein,* (NGI, Yeats archive, Box Y Mus, 25A, 1891-1925).
[37] *The Freeman,* (NGI, Yeats archive, Box Y Mus, 25A, 1891-1925).
[38] Delaney, 'Representations of the Travellers in the 1880s and 1900s', pp. 55-57.
[39] Yeats in a letter to John Quinn quoted in Homan Potterton, 'Jack B. Yeats and John Quinn' in *Irish Arts Review yearbook,* ix (1993), p.105. The letter is from a collection in the New York Public Library. Quinn was born in Ohio to Irish immigrant parents and

Figure. 3 *The Tinware Lass* (1913) – See Centrefold

In complete contrast to his harsh portrayal of men, Yeats' image of the Traveller woman is mainly one of youth, beauty and of a more wholesome character. Generally Yeats represented men more than women in his *oeuvre*; however, he did paint women more frequently up to the late 1920s. In a number of Yeats' paintings of the Traveller woman she is the medium between her community and the settled population. In the handcoloured Broadside print, *The Tinware lass* (1913), (Figure. 3) a young Traveller woman hawks the tin wares of the tinsmith. *Broadside* was a pamphlet comprising a one folded sheet of paper and contained three illustrations; some of which were accompanied by a ballad or poem. The Cuala press, run by Yeats' sisters Lily and Lolly, printed *Broadside* but Yeats had editorial control.[40] In this print a young Traveller woman carries a large sack of tin pots and basins slung over her shoulder selling the items door to door.[41] According to Artelia Court, a collector of Traveller folklore, it was the responsibility of the Traveller woman to create a relationship with the settled population and moreover to maintain it.[42] These 'diplomatic' relations created by the women were crucial for the trade of the tinsmith as they collected new business when selling the end product.[43] In this illustration the young Traveller girl is well dressed with a colourful blue and red check rug shawl and she has shoes on her feet.[44] This print reflects the reality of Traveller/sedentary relationships; if a Traveller woman was dressed respectably she had a better chance of successful dealings with housewives.

---

became a successful lawyer and patron of the arts. He collected works of art and literature from Europe but was particularly interested in Irish artists including Yeats, his father and brother.

[40] *Broadside* was issued monthly for seven years from 1908 to 1915 and even though it was a modern interpretation of the traditional balled sheets of the nineteenth century it was not a typical Irish publication. In these monthly *Broadsides* there were poems and ballads from England and Ireland juxtaposed with illustrations of characters like pirates, English Gypsies, tinkers and the rural Irish. Cuala Industries was set up by Yeats' sisters in 1908 and they specialized in the printing of art books. See Grifford Lewis, *The Yeats sisters and the Cuala* (Dublin, 1994).

[41] Reproduced in *Broadside* no.1, 6th year, June 1913. (Yeats archive, NGI, box 33)

[42] Court, *Puck of the Droms*, p.39.

[43] Ibid.

[44] The rug shawl had replaced the hooded shawl at the end of the nineteenth century and was mostly connected with Galway city and the surrounding area. Anne O'Dowd, *Common clothes and clothing* (Dublin, 1990), p.8.

Yeats' interest in the Traveller women intensified during his stay in Greystones, County Wicklow. Yeats and his wife moved permanently to Ireland in 1910 and lived in Greystones until his final move to Dublin in 1919. It was an uncertain time for the artist as he battled with depression, which resulted in a dramatic fall in work output. In a letter to Padric Colum (1881-1972) he referred to the isolation and lack of friends he experienced there and that the only connection to the outside world was from the tinkers that passed along the road.[45] This was the only lengthy period in his career when he lived in the Irish countryside, exposed to continual contact with Travellers. Even though he produced fewer paintings during the years 1913 to 1915 he constantly filled his sketchbooks. Evidence from these sketchbooks indicates a greater curiosity about the Traveller women than the men; he detailed what they wore and the babies they carried in their arms. As in the sketches *Tinker* (1915), (Figure. 4) and *Greystones Tinker* (1913), (Figure. 5) the women wear unusual clothes with big hats and full skirts.[46] The drawings from this period became looser and less detailed but they were more definite in the themes he noted, which were subsequently transferred into his oil paintings.[47] Indeed the contents of these sketchbooks were the basis for the tinker series of oils he produced in the 1920s.

Figure 4. *Tinker,* (1915).   Figure 5. *The Greystones Tinker,* (1913).
© Estate of Jack B. Yeats/ DACS 2006

---

[45] Yeats letter to Padric Colum quoted in Arnold, *Jack Yeats,* p.173.
[46] Jack B. Yeats, 'Tinker' 1915, from sketchbook 115 and 'Greystones Tinker' 1913, from sketchbook 103, Yeats archive, NGI.
[47] Hilary Pyle, *Jack B. Yeats: a biography* (Dublin, 1977), p. 114.

While living in Greystones, Yeats made the crucial change from watercolour to the medium of oil. In the painting *Tinker's fire* (1921), (Figure. 6) the colour intensified and he started to apply the paint more liberally with looser brushwork. In this painting Yeats touches on the domesticity of the tinker woman. The *Tinker's fire* is a scene where a woman and her small child are by a campfire and she is trying to break sticks for it on her knee. The small toddler, dressed in ragged garments with no shoes, is laughing in a contented manner. Yeats' idea for the composition of *Tinker's Fire* came from two sketches he made of a roadside tinker encampment in 1914. In the two pencil drawings, Yeats noted the horse and cart, and a woman collecting wood for the campfire with two figures seated around it. In the 1921 painting Yeats simply concentrates on the mother and child by the campfire. There is the added detail of a couple of pots and pans just behind the woman on the right-hand side of the painting and a horse saddle placed on the handle of a cart on the top right-hand corner.

Figure 6. *Tinker's Fire,* (1921) – See Centrefold

Arguably, Yeats' representation of the tinker woman in this painting indicates the background in which he grew up, that of the middle class, where the Victorian ideology of femininity was 'built on a platform of moral respectability and domesticity'.[48] This is evident in the *Tinker's Fire* as the symbol of the child emphasises the role of this woman as a mother, while the pots to the left create a domestic space by the campfire. Traditionally, Victorian women were placed in 'domestic paintings', which represented women in their dutiful roles as carers and teachers of children but also engaged in activities like sewing, reading, sitting in a garden or interior space.[49] Domestic scenes in paintings were important in shaping 'middle-class identity and in regulating sexual and class differences' and they were directed specifically at middle-class tastes.[50] But the difference in *Tinker's Fire* to the mother and child portraits by his Irish contemporaries, Sir William Orpen and John Lavery, is that the child is not sitting on its mother's lap but placed on the ground. The baby on the ground draws attention to the uncertainty of a home with no physical boundaries yet the issue of poverty and homelessness is clearly romanticised in this painting.

---

[48] Lynda Nead, 'Class and sexuality in Victorian art' in Gill Perry (ed.), *Art and its histories. Gender and art* (London, 1999), p.154.

[49] Deborah Cherry, *Painting women. Victorian women artists* (London, 1993), p. 120. 'Domestic paintings' were created by both male and female artists.

[50] Cherry, *Painting women,* p. 120.

The rural people were reluctant to give a free night's lodgings to the tinkers; it was usually in exchange for services. In Lady Gregory's study on the Travellers, *The Wandering Tribe,* published in 1903, she interviewed people from the settled community about the Travellers. One observer explained that the tinkers themselves would have abhorred taking a night's shelter inside the home of a rural peasant, as they did not want to sleep in a bed claiming 'they would never be any good after' and found sleeping outside healthier.[51] As noted by Jeanne Flood in her examination of Synge's play *The Tinker's Wedding,* the tinkers 'live at ease in nature, neither having nor needing a shelter'[52] and so too in Yeats' work his tinkers are rarely represented with shelter. This perhaps indicates Yeats' refusal to see a tent or a caravan as shelter in any real sense. Generally the Travellers would have had their own means of shelter with them like a makeshift tent or caravan.

A year after *Tinker's Fire* he painted, *Tinkers, Early Morning,* (1922), and according to Arnold it is a particularly strong canvas from this period.[53] It draws on the recurrent symbols for both sexes, the idealization of a young Traveller woman and the stylised face of the older man. The man, depicted as dark and sinister, looks defiantly out towards the viewer while the young woman has her back to the viewer and her pose is reminiscent of a classical 'antique' statue. The strong morning light casts shadows on the lane, placing both the male Traveller and the water pump in the shade. Similar to the painting *Tinker's Fire* there are two identifiable sketches quickly drawn in a sketchbook from 1914 that were the source for this work. The first sketch focused solely on the grace and poise of the young woman. The second, he titled *'Tinker washing herself'* (Figure. 7) and with both the male and female characters it was the composition he drew upon for *Tinkers, Early morning*. In these sketches Yeats was capturing a young tinker woman carrying out her morning wash at the pump. In the finished oil painting of 1922, Yeats changed the title and greatly obscured the water pump. Both the *Tinker's Fire* and *Tinkers, Early Morning* were exhibited in Dublin immediately after they were painted but were not purchased until the early 1940s.[54]

---

[51] Lady Gregory, 'The Wandering Tribe' (1903) reprinted in *Poets and dreamers: studies and translations from the Irish* (New York, Coole edition, 1974), p.95.
[52] Jeanne Flood, 'Thematic variations in Synge's early peasant plays' in *Eire-Ireland*, vii (1972), p. 75.
[53] Arnold, *Jack Yeats*, p.208.
[54] Christie's London, *The Irish Sale,* (22 May, 1998), lot no. 112 and Sotheby's, London, (16 May, 1996), lot no. 490.

Figure 7. *Tinker Washing Herself* (1914).
© Estate of Jack B. Yeats/ DACS 2006

Yeats chose to paint the polar opposite to his own middle-class background and he showed a persistent fascination with the 'other', beginning with the Gypsies in Devon in 1897. Both Yeats and Synge also found the 'other' in the peasants of the west of Ireland and Yeats was one of the first artists to give them a genuine visual representation in art.[55] It was feasible that Yeats and Synge came across Travellers on their trip around the west in 1905, as Yeats created the two watercolours *A Tinker* and *The Tinker's Curse* in the same year. However, painting the Irish Travellers or English Gypsies in a community group with their tents and caravans was not of a particular interest to Yeats.

Yeats boldly used 'Tinker' liberally in his titles to distinguish between rural peasants who dressed, particularly the women, in a similar fashion. Travellers were used as subject matter in the publication *Broadside,* which was bought and read by the middle and upper classes in Irish society.[56] The Traveller's inclusion

---

[55] Cyril Barrett and Jeanne Sheehy, 'Visual arts and society, 1850-1900' in W.E Vaughan (ed.), *A new history of Ireland. VI, Ireland under the union II-1870-1921* (Oxford, 1996), p. 487.
[56] The patrons of the Cuala Press came from the Protestant landed gentry and they were the main regular subscribers for books and *Broadsides* over a number of years. Joan Hardwick, *The Yeats sisters: a biography of Susan and Elizabeth Yeats* (London, 1996), pp 162-163.

in this light-hearted publication, which had many characters including pirates, jockeys, and circus people, highlights how Yeats saw the Travellers as 'fantastical' characters and perhaps more appealing to him than the Irish peasant. As Arnold suggests; this publication was not intended to be 'representative Irish' and was a more creative and artistic endeavour.[57]

Yeats' representation of the Traveller woman was more sympathetic than the Traveller male, since he tended to focus on their ways and means of gaining an income; although, begging (an important source of income) was not represented. Even though the settled population are not present with the Travellers in many of his paintings, in the print *The Tinware Lass,* the viewer assumes the young woman will be in contact with rural housewives in door-to-door selling. In this print, without the help of the caption, it would be difficult to interpret the image as a Traveller woman and it appears that Yeats was interested in how the Traveller figure appeared similar to the Irish in general. This is in contrast to Synge's written accounts of Traveller women, where he describes them as being different not only in manner but in physical appearance. Synge spoke of fair day stalls thus: 'They are attended to by the semi-gypsy or tinker class among [whom] women with curiously Mongolian features are not rare'.[58] Synge's view of the Travellers was not an unusual one and as Burke asserts, 'itinerants and sub-cultures in the British Isles in the nineteenth century became increasingly subject to a process of orientalization'.[59]

During the 1920s, Ireland was struggling along its path to becoming a modern Free State and Irish artists, including Seán Keating (1889-1977), were representing these nationalist aspirations in their paintings.[60] The Irish Free State grew increasingly concerned about the problems arising from the destitute poor. The Travellers, a marginal group, were in conflict with the new idealism of Irish nationalism and in the era of modernisation, there was less use for a non-contributing class. In contrast to Keating's work of the Free State infrastructure, Yeats' images of the Irish Travellers were probably not a desired

---

[57] Arnold, *Jack Yeats,* p.169.
[58] J.M Synge, 'The vagrants in Wicklow' in Alan Price, *J.M Synge: collected works, II, prose* (Oxford, 1966), pp 197-198.
[59] Burke, 'Eighteenth-century European scholarship and nineteenth century Irish literature', p. 210.
[60] Cullen, *Visual politics: the representation of Ireland,* p. 163. Keating's work includes the on site paintings and drawings of construction of the Hydro-electric power station in Poulaphouca. See Andy Bielenberg, 'Seán Keating, the Shannon scheme and the art of State-building' in Andy Bielenberg (ed.), *The Shannon scheme and the electrification of the Irish Free State* (Dublin, 2002).

subject matter for the rising, Catholic, bourgeois consumer. In Yeats' work a shift occurred in his perception and representation of the Irish Travellers, which began with the sketchbooks, complied in Greystones. Still retaining the harsh image of the male Traveller, Yeats seemed more willing to explore their isolation in Irish society and they cut a lonelier yet more dignified figure in his paintings of the 1920s.[61] Yeats viewed the Irish Travellers differently from the Literary Revivalists who were attracted to the bohemianism of the Traveller lifestyle. He was fascinated with them as a group that shared characteristics with the general population but were also a unique people and culture within the rural community. The Traveller was a sporadic but persistent theme that ran through his entire career and it emanated from a great degree of admiration. He considered them a worthy subject matter at a time when it was not commercially viable or popular. In fact from the 1930s to the 1950s the wandering figure emerged as a very powerful symbol in his work.[62]

---

[61] S.B Kennedy, *Irish art and modernism, 1880-1950* (Belfast, 1991), p. 27.
[62] For example *Death for Only One* (1938), *Two Men Walking* (1946), *A Place of Islands* (1946), *On Through the Silent Lands* (1951) and *The Plank Road* (1955). Yeats described *Death for Only One* as 'of a dead tramp lying on a headland with another tramp standing by ... and a dark sea and dark sky'. Yeats in a letter to Thomas MacGreevy quoted in Arnold, *Jack Yeats,* p. 280.

CHAPTER FOUR

PRIVILEGED PERSPECTIVES
AND SUBVERTED TYPES:
JAMES STEPHENS' '*THE DEMI-GODS*'

PAUL DELANEY

Irish writers have expressed a pronounced interest in Travellers for over a century, and this interest has been registered in a variety of forms, including poetry, drama and prose fiction. Specifically delineated Traveller characters in literature (rather than generally defined vagrants or the landless poor) can be traced back at least as far as William Carleton's *The Emigrants of Ahadarra*, which was published in 1848. More recently John Millington Synge, William Butler Yeats, Lady Gregory, Douglas Hyde, Thomas MacDonagh, Pádraic Ó Conaire, Seumas O'Kelly, Liam O'Flaherty, Seán O'Faoláin, John B. Keane, Bryan MacMahon, Patrick Kavanagh, Sigerson Clifford, Patricia Lynch, Jennifer Johnston, Richard Murphy, Éilís Ní Dhuibhne, Brian Moore, Mary Ryan and Marina Carr are just some of the writers who have drawn on a wealth of beliefs and superstitions in their depictions of this minority. According to the critic Robert E. Rhodes, each of these writers has drawn on elements of a 'received lore' about Travellers for a variety of effects and purposes.[1] In many instances, Travellers have been represented according to type and Traveller characters have been made to fit a generic image. Many characteristics are typically associated with this image including violence, promiscuity, drunkenness, theft, poverty, cunning, lawlessness, primitiveness, taciturnity and loquaciousness. Some writers have been sympathetic in their portraits and have afforded Travellers a privileged place in their work. Others have been less favourably disposed and have drawn sketches which are reductive, degrading or

---

[1] Robert E. Rhodes, '"More matter for a May morning": J.M. Synge's *The Tinker's wedding*', in A. G. Gonzalez, (ed.), *Assessing the achievement of J.M. Synge* (Westport, 1996), p. 108

condescending. Either way, a substantial body of writers has contributed to what might be termed 'a discourse on nomadism' in Irish writing.

As a member of the settled community, what interests me about this is firstly that so many settled authors have felt the necessity to represent Travellers in their work, particularly over the last hundred years, and secondly that these representations are various enough to hint at the interests of their authors and the time in which they were effected. There is a sense that many of the changes in Irish society – as well as many of the fears and much of the excitement which has attended these changes – have been explored through the figure of the Traveller. Debates about property, labour and social welfare have been played out at the Traveller-settled interface, for instance, as have questions relating to censorship, independence and the nature of 'freedom'. Travellers have also been used to sound out discussions about wealth and status, and they have often been deployed as a foil to register changing attitudes towards religion, modernity, sex and the environment. Given the variety of uses to which their representation has been put, it could be argued that Travellers have been granted a signifying potential in Irish writing that changes in accordance with the needs and interests of the writer in question.

The pages that follow explore the work of one settled author, James Stephens, who engaged with the presence of Travellers in his writing. In particular, the focus is on one of Stephens' earlier novels, *The Demi-Gods*, which was published in 1914 and later adapted for – but never performed on – the stage. My reasons for this choice are several. For one thing, Stephens' portrayal of Travellers was largely sympathetic and utilized representative strategies which undermined the received opinions and preconceived prejudices of his day. For another thing, Stephens' engagement was conditioned by other interests (most notably, his critique of capitalism and middle-class 'settled' society), and in many respects he can be said to offer a good example of the way in which the figure of the Traveller is sometimes used as a metaphor for the expression of other – private or public – questions and concerns. Furthermore, many of Stephens' depictions are seductive and multifaceted, and give the lie to any easy reading which claims that all representations of Travellers by settled authors are inherently reductive and racist.

James Stephens was born in Dublin in either 1880 or 1882. Little is known for certain about his early years (not least because Stephens himself invented a series of complex, contradictory stories in his later life), but the little that is known suggests a life of poverty and deprivation. He was orphaned at a young age and sent to the Meath Protestant Industrial School, probably at the age of four; he remained there until 1896, when he obtained a post as a solicitor's clerk in Dublin. He worked as a low paid clerk – a job he detested – for the next sixteen years. His *annus mirabilis*, 1912, saw the publication of his first two novels, *The Charwoman's Daughter* and *The Crock of Gold*, and also marked the appearance of his second collection of poetry, *The Hill of Vision*. The two novels, in particular, were well received and Stephens subsequently earned his living as a writer and critic. He served as registrar of the National Gallery of Ireland from 1915 to 1925, and spent much of his later life in London, where he worked as a broadcaster for the BBC. He died in 1950.

If little is known for certain about Stephens' early years, it is nonetheless quite clear that he was an avid reader of mystical writers like George Russell and Madame Blavatsky. Transcendentalism and Theosophy provided a long-standing influence on his writing career, and from the outset his work was informed by the Theosophist belief that men and women are comprised of a triune state of being (body, soul and spirit) which must be brought into some kind of harmony. Stephens celebrated qualities that were central to Blavatsky's teachings, such as charity, goodwill and kindness, and he also placed considerable emphasis on the Theosophist principle that the universe was created by the conflict of antinomies or opposites – man/woman, night/day, good/evil, etc. Stephens also supported the idea that it was through the conflict of these antinomies that the universal energies were eternally generated.[2] In addition to Blavatsky and the Theosophists, Stephens was also impressed by the work of the Romantic poet William Blake. He was particularly attracted to Blake's famous maxim that 'without contraries is no progression', and the argument that 'attraction and repulsion, reason and energy, love and hate, are necessary to human existence' is exemplified in many of Stephens' texts.[3] The influence of Blake can also be detected in Stephens' condemnation of materialism and authority, as well as in his critique of organised religion and his celebration of childhood. Blake's idiosyncratic use of symbolism and myth provided a further impression on Stephens, and the Romantic poet's precepts regarding the apotheosis of the imagination and the doctrine of 'god in man' were to have a lasting influence on the Irish writer.[4]

---

[2] Patricia McFate, *The Writings of James Stephens: variations on a theme of love* (London, 1979), p. 11; Augustine Martin, *James Stephens: A Critical Study* (Dublin, 1977), pp 35-36
[3] William Blake, 'The marriage of heaven and hell', W.H. Stevenson (ed.) *The poems of William Blake* (London, 1971), p. 105
[4] For an extended discussion of the influence of Blake, see Hilary Pyle, *James Stephens: his work and an account of his life* (London, 1965), Chapters 3 and 4.

Privileged Perspectives and Subverted Types: James Stephens '*The Demi-Gods*'

Although Stephens was influenced by Blake and the Theosophists, that influence was neither reductive nor uncritical. Instead, as the foremost Stephens scholar Augustine Martin has shown, Stephens 'made his own of his sources' and 'absorbed from Blake and Blavatsky those patterns of myth, doctrine and symbology which responded to … his creative talent' in order to make 'an imaginative world recognisably and vividly his own'.[5] One of the things which are distinctive about this 'imaginative world' is the way that it collapses distinctions which readers might otherwise take for granted. The conventions which distinguish different forms and styles of writing, for instance, are repeatedly transgressed in Stephens' work, and the reading experience can often appear unsettling as a result. Realism blends into fantasy in much of his fiction, and popular literature is interleaved with mysticism and high art. Moreover, comedy is frequently used to counterpoint or parallel serious themes and concerns, and Stephens' tone often modulates between solemnity and parody – indeed, it often appears to be both at the same time. His writing also incorporates and conflates elements of prophecy, satire, fable, legend and farce. To quote Martin once again, counterpoint is 'a consistent feature of Stephens' narrative strategy', which enabled him to write extraordinary characters into quotidian settings and to juxtapose cosmic events with domestic concerns.[6] As Martin suggests, this strategy has obvious comic potential and is common to all of Stephens' prose fictions. Nowhere, however, is it more apparent than in the design of his third novel, *The Demi-Gods*.

In *The Demi-Gods*, three angels with Celtic names – Finaun, Caeltia and Art – descend from heaven and enter into companionship with two Travellers, Patsy Mac Cann and his daughter Mary. The angels are keen to learn about life on earth and to pass as ordinary individuals. To that end, they shed their wings and crowns and put on the clothes that Patsy offers them. Their subsequent adventures take them along minor rural paths, from Donegal through Connemara to Kerry, before they return full circle at the story's close. In the course of their travels they meet several other characters, including Eileen Ni Cooley (a tempestuous Traveller with a string of lovers, including Patsy) and Billy the Music (a travelling concertina player who was formerly a settled farmer called Old Carolan). They also come across a fallen seraph in drag (the legendary Irish hero Cuchulain), and a tormented Kerryman (Brien O'Brien) who has been evicted from hell and who was a powerful magician in a previous life. As the story develops it becomes clear that each of the angels is associated with a particular Traveller – Finaun is paired with Eileen, Caeltia with Patsy,

---

[5] Martin, *James Stephens*, p. 37
[6] Ibid., p. 46

and Art with Mary – and there is a suggestion that the angels are guardian angels in the Christian sense of the word. It is characteristic of Stephens, however, to resist any rigid identification with doctrine, so it is also hinted that the relationship between the angels and the Travellers accords with the Theosophist belief that everything on earth has its celestial counterpart.

Although Travellers are paired with angels in *The Demi-Gods*, however, this is not to suggest that Patsy, Eileen or Mary should be considered impossibly virtuous or that their lifestyle is romanticized or rendered idyllic by Stephens. On the contrary, life on the road is characterized by neglect, hunger and the cold, and this takes its toll on those who are poor and most vulnerable. The slightest of comments by the narrator makes this point poignantly clear. Early in the narrative Stephens includes a brief account of the Mac Cann family history. It is mentioned that Mary had a mother and several brothers and sisters, but that each of '(the others had died wintry deaths)'.[7] Nothing more is said about these characters, and Patsy's wife and most of his children are left without a name. The tone of Stephens' narrative is understated at this point – the reference is only included in brackets, in a passing parenthesis – but the implication is clear: life on the road is a constant struggle for survival, and Patsy, Eileen and Mary must be tough if they are to stay alive. The two older Travellers, in particular, are sketched with the boldest of strokes by Stephens – Patsy appears as a bullish patriarch and an adept thief, and Eileen is afforded a reputation for promiscuity and feistiness. (Mary pales in comparison to either of these vibrant, vital characters, although she holds her own in her frequent quarrels with her father.) Stephens' portrait of these characters is such that it could be argued that they embody many of the defining features of the traditional anti-nomadic type. They endlessly scrap and steal, for instance, and they are passionate and shameless; they are also placed beyond the pale of polite society, and their speech is punctuated with a certain licence and the occasional curse. What is more, their lives are said to be governed by different codes of conduct – the narrator goes so far as to remark that 'within an organized humanity [they] might almost have been reckoned as a different species' – and they are even described as being animal-like in manner and appearance.[8] Mary is variously made to resemble a cat, a bird, a panther and a deer, while Patsy is related to any number of animals, including a wolf, a vulture, a bear, a fish, a dog and a sheep.

However, Stephens resists any ready-made associations between 'tinkers' and animals in *The Demi-Gods* by anthropomorphizing anything that is not human

---

[7] James Stephens, *The Demi-Gods* (1914; rprt., Dublin, 1982), p. 54
[8] Ibid., p. 46

and by investing all forms of life with personality and psychic energy. All life is cosmically interrelated in this book (hence the repeated references to reincarnation), so it is more than appropriate that the Travellers should converse with and resemble animals. Stephens also resists any ready-made equation of 'tinkers' and animals by associating other characters with the natural world – Art talks to a spider in one of the funniest episodes in the book, Finaun shares Mary's close connection with the Mac Canns' donkey, and the narrator enters the story (in a particularly bizarre chapter) to chat with this much-abused animal. Stephens goes further, however, in his engagement with the standard racist formulation of the 'tinker-as-animal', for he provides the reader with a radical counter perspective with which to challenge the traditional equation. When describing the relationship between the Travellers and the settled community, the narrator remarks:

> For the vagabonds these people did not count; Mac Cann and his daughter scarcely looked on them as human beings, and if he had generalised about them at all, he would have said that there was no difference between these folk and the trees that shaded their dwellings in leafy spray, that they were rooted in their houses, and that they had no idea of life other than the trees might have which snuff for ever the same atmosphere and look on the same horizon until they droop again to the clay they lifted from.[9]

Stephens privileges this perspective in *The Demi-Gods* and uses it to question the basic humanity of the larger settled community. He also uses it to reverse the popular image of the Travellers as foul-mouthed and vicious, and to cast members of settled society in standard 'tinker-like' roles. On more than one occasion, for example, the reader is informed that 'the language of [settled folk] was seldom gracious' and that their behaviour was ugly and hostile.[10] Stephens privileges this perspective because it gives him access to a range of opinions which are otherwise unfamiliar and it enables him to depict recognizable characters (that is to say, other settled characters) in ways which are challenging and estranging. Indeed, the reader is told that Patsy knew settled folk 'from an angle at which they seldom caught themselves or each other', and it is this angle which is given authority in *The Demi-Gods*.[11] It is crucial that the angels share the perspective and the experience of the Travellers ('to the angels', the narrator notes, the people they met on the roads 'were humanity, and the others were, they did not know what'), and that this is not disputed in any significant way in the text.[12]

---

[9] Ibid., p. 52
[10] Ibid., p. 52
[11] Ibid., p. 48
[12] Ibid., p. 53

Significantly, very few members of the settled populace appear in *The Demi-Gods*, and those that are presented are deeply problematic. Old Carolan (before he becomes the carefree Billy the Music), Brien O'Brien (in his most recent incarnation), and the unnamed couple in the Big House (in a slightly anomalous late chapter) provide the fullest representations of settled life in the book. However, none of these characters are agreeable – Old Carolan is a miser, Brien O'Brien is a truculent bully, and the Big House couple are pallid and deceitful – and none of them offers a perspective that challenges the beliefs of either the angels or the Travellers. Moreover, the angels partake in unexpected – that is to say, unconventional or stereotypically 'tinker-like' – forms of behaviour throughout this book. In the course of their travels, they smoke freely, drink deeply and join in the occasional fight; they also dress in the clothes that Patsy has pinched and share the food that he steals. Caeltia even helps Mary to steal food at a late stage in the novel, taking as justification her simple assertion 'one must eat'.[13] At no point do they demonstrate any interest in the larger settled community, nor do they express any qualms about committing these acts. Instead, the narrator exploits the comic potential of placing Travellers alongside angels, and Stephens revels in the opportunity of refusing – and indeed deconstructing – traditional preconceptions and prejudices.

In his short documentary about life in the capital during Easter Week 1916, *The Insurrection in Dublin*, Stephens advanced the argument that 'laughter is the sole excess that is wholesome'.[14] This idea was a favourite of his and was repeated on a number of other occasions. It finds its fullest expression in *The Demi-Gods* when Finaun remarks that 'humour is the health of the mind'.[15] Humour is wholesome or healthy for Stephens because it provides a safety valve of sorts, and allows pieties and prejudices to be challenged and reinterpreted in a spirit of irony and irreverence. It also provides a vehicle for the expression of themes and concerns which might otherwise be deemed sinister or taboo. This is a point worth stressing because *The Demi-Gods*, for all its irreverence and comic invention, is a novel with a serious edge. Central to Stephens' book is the critique of capitalism and the desire for possession, and an identification of the many lines of association between property, power, justice, love and greed. Each of these themes is integral to the design of the book, with love afforded a special prominence which is in accordance with Stephens' other fictions.

---

[13] Ibid., p. 148
[14] James Stephens, *The Insurrection in Dublin* (1916; rprt., London, 1965), p. 10
[15] Stephens, *Demi-Gods*, p. 133

Love is opposed to possession in *The Demi-Gods*, and one of the lessons that the Travellers – and Patsy in particular – must learn involves the dangers of avarice and material greed. This is illustrated, perhaps most vividly, in the third section of the novel with the story of Billy the Music. Billy is a wandering musician who tells a cautionary tale. Until recently he was a successful farmer who became so obsessed by the desire for wealth that he shirked his responsibilities as a husband, an employer and a father. Indeed, Billy's desire for wealth led him to brutalize everyone he once knew – Patsy voices the common belief that Billy's sister committed suicide as a result of his behaviour, and it is also chillingly reported that he 'used to starve the stomach out' of his wife and children.[16] His workers fared no better, and Billy recalls the lengths he took to cheat and abuse those who laboured on his farm. As he relates his story, Billy demonstrates that he is under no illusions about the source of his former power. 'Of course I knew that [the labourers] didn't want to work for me,' he admits, 'and that, bating the hunger, they'd have seen me far enough before they'd lift a hand for my good; but I had them by the hasp, for as long as men have to eat, any man with the food can make them do whatever he wants them to do'.[17] Billy's point is depressingly obvious (wealth equals power), and it is suggestive of a theme which preoccupied Stephens throughout his career.

Much of Stephens' best work offers an effective criticism of capitalism, and the relationship between employers and workers was a topic which he returned to time and again in his poetry and his fiction. Invariably, Stephens saw the relationship as abusive and degrading. An early poem, 'To The Four Courts, Please' (published in his first collection, *Insurrections* [1909]), signalled Stephens' intent, and painted a brutal portrait of an old cabby who was severely debilitated by a life of poverty. In Stephens' poem, work and malnourishment have left their mark on the old man (his eyes are pouched, his skin is discoloured and his mouth is lop-sided), and his horse has been similarly scarred by neglect and hard labour (its knees are 'knuckly', its ears are limp and its chest is 'ribbed and forked'). Nonetheless, man and horse must continue to slave for those with money, for the simple reason that 'the poor, when they're old, have little peace'.[18] Similar concerns were raised in early poems like 'The Dancer', where a woman refuses to prostitute herself and dance for a drunken mob, and 'Fifty Pounds a Year and a Pension', where the wasted life of a clerk is bitterly chronicled.

---

[16] Ibid., p. 100
[17] Ibid., p. 104
[18] James Stephens, 'To the Four Courts, Please', *Insurrections* (Dublin., 1909), p 33

This critique of capitalism was reiterated in Stephens' early prose fiction. His much-loved debut novel, *The Charwoman's Daughter*, which is widely considered the first work of fiction to deal with life in the Dublin slums, sketched the consequences of exploitation, drudgery and unemployment among the working class and argued that 'there is really only one grave and debasing vice in the world, and that is poverty'.[19] Stephens' critique also found expression in his comic masterpiece, *The Crock of Gold*, through the interpolated stories of the two clerks, and was forcefully articulated in his harrowing short story 'Hunger' (1918), which mercilessly recorded the slow starvation of an entire family in the aftermath of the 1913 Lockout. In 'Hunger' the established system of wage-labour leads to distress, starvation and suffering. What is more, in *The Charwoman's Daughter* it exerts a very real pressure on the inhabitants of the tenements and results in all kinds of anguish.

However, hunger isn't always a physical experience in Stephens' work – sometimes it is invested with a figurative or a metaphorical significance. In spite of the problems it causes the Makebelieve family, for instance, hunger is also ascribed positive characteristics in *The Charwoman's Daughter*. The narrator associates it with 'life, ambition, goodwill and understanding', and sets this against 'fullness', which he claims is replete with 'all those negatives which culminate in greediness, stupidity and decay'.[20] This idea resurfaces in *The Crock of Gold*, where 'hunger and love and curiosity' are judged 'the great impelling forces of life', and one of the characters opines that 'every person who is hungry is a good person and every person who is not hungry is a bad person'.[21] To be hungry is to be benign or generous in both of these texts because it is equated with being openhearted and open-minded – basically, it is to have an appetite. To be full, on the other hand, is to be arrogant and avaricious because it demonstrates greed and a preoccupation with the self. It is perhaps not surprising that this argument has occasioned unease among many Stephens scholars, and it has sometimes been cited as evidence of a disturbing 'conjunction of heroism and victimization' in his work.[22]

Many readers have expressed concern that the experience of hunger is often divorced from the reality of pain and suffering in Stephens' work ('Hunger' is the obvious exception to this argument), and that it is instead invested with a reassuring aesthetic or symbolic significance. At the same time, readers have

---

[19] James Stephens, *The Charwoman's Daughter* (1912; rprt., Dublin, 1972), p. 87
[20] Ibid., p. 126
[21] James Stephens, *The Crock of Gold* (1912; rprt., Dublin, 1995), pp 7, 67
[22] John Wilson Foster, *Fictions of the Irish literary revival: a changeling art* (Dublin, 1987), p. 258

noted that victims of hunger are often raised to the status of heroes or martyrs in his texts because of their capacity to reach out to others and endure. *The Demi-Gods* fits this pattern in part, but it differs from Stephens' other early novels by not claiming any of its characters as heroic. Patsy and Eileen are loveable rogues but they hardly attain heroic status in the course of their travels. The same can be said for the other key characters in the book. Indeed, the only hero who is included in Stephens' novel – the legendary warrior Cuchulain, who was the great inspiration of the Literary Revival – is made to play a debased or comic part. Patsy describes him, somewhat irreverently, as 'a dandy lad that never got his hair cut since he was a mother's boy', and the narrator portrays him as a fallen seraph with a violent streak.[23] It would appear that abstract concepts like heroism hold little attraction for the Travellers (at least in the mind of Stephens), as they are faced with the day-to-day struggle for survival. It is appropriate, therefore, that such concepts are written out of Stephens' text.

Hunger is certainly a defining feature of life on the roads in *The Demi-Gods*. It is considered the primary reason behind the Travellers' journey through Ireland and from the outset every aspect of the Mac Canns' life seems to be determined by the search for food. The narrator notes as much when he comments that the angels and the Travellers 'continued their travels' – or rather, 'it would be more correct to say they continued their search for food, for that in reality was the objective of each day's journeying'.[24] Food is a great preoccupation in *The Demi-Gods*, and the text is stuffed with references to vegetables, bread, cheese, meat and drink. Food is also a mainstay of conversation, and the narrator is of the opinion that 'the hunt for food' was Patsy's 'one occupation, and it was an engrossing one'.[25] Food is first alluded to in the opening page of the story, when Patsy declares his 'wish ... that Christian people were able to eat grass like the beasts' since 'then there wouldn't be any more trouble in the world'. Patsy continues with this line of thought in the succeeding lines of the opening chapter ('if every person had enough to eat there'd be no more trouble and we could fight our fill'), and it gradually becomes clear that this opinion is shared by the narrator of *The Demi-Gods*.[26] However, resources are not evenly shared in this world and all of the characters experience hunger in the course of their travels. As Mary explains to the angels (when they attempt to realize Patsy's 'wish'), 'every kind of animal eats [grass], but Christians don't ... I never heard tell of

---

[23] Stephens, *Demi-Gods*, p. 113
[24] Ibid., p. 97
[25] Ibid., p. 47
[26] Ibid., p. 18

any person that ate grass except that they were dying of the hunger and couldn't help themselves, poor creatures!'[27]

Hunger evokes painful echoes of famine in the above quotation. However, elsewhere in the text it leads to extraordinary acts of trickery and theft. For most of the story, Patsy keeps the small band of Travellers and angels together by means of subterfuge and cunning (or by 'cleverly' stealing from those he meets), and Mary replicates her father's actions when he briefly parts way with the group in the fourth section of the text.[28] It is significant that the narrator describes these actions as instances of 'skill and activity', and he is unambiguous in his assertion that Patsy and Mary merit 'praise' for the way that they manage to survive.[29] This is because the characteristics that Stephens ascribes to the Travellers – of theft, mobility and trespass – are inimical to the values of any settled materialist society. That Stephens supports the Mac Canns in their subversion of these values is clear from a short episode which occurs in the closing pages of the book. As the band of characters wind their way back to Knockbeg, and to the point from whence they started their journey, Caeltia solemnly remarks 'robbery is infantile and of no importance'. Caeltia's comments provoke a short discussion, in which Patsy's contribution is telling. The reader is informed that Patsy 'replied cunningly ... "it fills the stomach"', and it is clear from what follows that he has the better of the argument. Caeltia, after all, has profited from acts of theft on a number of occasions, and the whiff of hypocrisy compels him to revise his opinion. 'The stomach has to be filled', he concedes, 'its filling is a necessity superior to any proprietorial right or disciplinary ethic'.[30] The incident is of minor significance in the tale, but the point is vital to the larger message of *The Demi-Gods*. It is also central to Stephens' use of the Traveller figure in this book. For Stephens' Travellers are ultimately depicted as vibrant, slippery characters who are at odds with the ethics of an increasingly capitalist Ireland. His Travellers confound the received way of conceiving relations in the world and offer a perspective on this world which differs from those around them. It is for this reason that they are cherished by the narrator.

Once again, Travellers and angels are equated in a number of ways in *The Demi-Gods*. They are related physically, temperamentally and instinctually, and they are also made to share certain orthodox Christian and Theosophist links. Significantly, they also share some rather unexpected moral sensibilities – even

---

[27] Ibid., p. 37
[28] Ibid., p. 47
[29] Ibid., p. 148
[30] Ibid., pp 182-183

though the narrator (somewhat paradoxically) is of the opinion that Patsy considered morality, like law and religion, as 'something to be avoided'.[31] 'It is to be remarked that the angels were strangely like Patsy Mac Cann', the narrator announces at one point:

> Their ideas of right and wrong almost entirely coincided with his. They had no property and so they had no prejudices, for the person who has nothing may look upon the world as his inheritance, while the person who has something has seldom anything but that.
> Civilization, having built itself upon the Rights of Property, has sought on many occasions to unbuild itself again in sheer desperation of any advance, but from the great Ethic of Possession there never has been any escape, and there never will be until the solidarity of man has been really created, and until man ceases to see the wolf in his neighbour.[32]

As Patricia McFate has noted, 'it is the desire to possess another' person which leads to all kinds of problems in Stephens' work.[33] Characters who are proprietorial or possessive invariably restrict the potential of those around them. In *The Charwoman's Daughter*, Mary must find some way to escape her mother's overprotective fantasies if she is to ever grow up; she must also reject the attention of the policeman who seeks to dominate her and subject her to his will. This pattern is repeated in Stephens' other prose narratives, and gains special significance in *The Demi-Gods* in the stories of Brien O'Brien and Old Carolan/Billy the Music. Both of these stories suggest the dangers of greed and materialism, and both of them illustrate some of the ways that wealth can be used to debase and humiliate those who have nothing. When Billy the Music describes how he used to exploit his workers, for example, Patsy remarks, 'if I was one of your men ... you wouldn't have treated me that way ... for I'd have broken your skull with a spade'. Patsy's comments draw a 'mild', sardonic response from Billy the Music:

> If you had been one of my men you'd have been as tame as a little kitten; you'd have crawled round me with your hat in your hand and your eyes turned up like a dying duck's, and you'd have said, 'Yes, sir,' and 'No, sir,' like the other men that I welted the stuffing out of with my two fists, and broke the spirits of with labour and hunger. Don't be talking now, for you're an ignorant man in these things.[34]

---

[31] Ibid., p. 46
[32] Ibid., p. 50
[33] McFate, *Writings of James Stephens*, p. 152
[34] Stephens, *Demi-Gods*, p. 107

Patsy refuses to be cowed and 'triumphantly' reminds Billy the Music that he stole a pair of boots and a hen from him in a previous encounter. However, it is Billy the Music's terrible words which leave the longest impression.

If the power to possess corresponds with the power to render abject on this occasion, Brien O'Brien and Billy the Music also demonstrate that the desire for possession has terrible consequences for those in positions of power. It is clear from both stories that any attempt at possession – whether it is possession of another person, their labour or their body – results in the brutalization of the self and psyche. In this respect, Stephens might be said (albeit by chance, perhaps) to recall the words of Frederick Douglass, the great African-American writer and political agitator, who diagnosed 'the brutalizing effects of slavery upon *both* slave and slaveholder'.[35] Although Douglass's comments were made in an entirely different context – as part of the abolitionist debate in mid-nineteenth century America – they nonetheless have a certain resonance here, since slavery and wage-labour were synonymous for Stephens and employers were often depicted as slave-owners in his work. Old Carolan learns this lesson, which is why he abandons his fortune, changes his name and takes to the road; Brien O'Brien does not, which is why he is destined to remain a brute who will be reincarnated at a low level in the next life. Patsy must also learn this lesson if he is to avoid the temptation of property (a temptation which he almost succumbs to late in the novel), and cease to be the 'domineering man' that Eileen fears to love.[36]

The Demi-Gods provides an effective – enjoyable – critique of any order based on prudence and possession, and it is for this reason that Martin has described it as 'an implicit celebration of the Dionysian[37] principle in man, his tendency towards passion, imagination and excess'.[38] This description succinctly registers various issues which are woven into the text of *The Demi-Gods*, and it can also be used to sum up many of the themes and concerns which are explored in the novel *The Crock of Gold*. In *The Crock of Gold*, Stephens contrasts a pastoral world of movement, freedom and nature with (and here there are echoes of Blake) a cityscape of laws, regulations and loneliness. What is more, in both

---

[35] Frederick Douglass, *Narrative of the life of Frederick Douglass, an American slave, written by himself*, William L. Andrews and William S. McFeely (eds.), (1845; rprt., New York, 1997), p. 36 [emphasis added]
[36] Stephens, *Demi-Gods*, p. 78
[37] *The Oxford Dictionary of English* (2nd edn, Oxford, 2003), p. 490. It defines Dionysian or Dionysiac as 'relating to the god Dionysius; [also] relating to the sensual, spontaneous and emotional aspects of human nature.'
[38] Martin, *James Stephens*, p. 76

texts he issues a plea for passion and transgression, and on both occasions he links this to a celebration of desire and the body. This celebration is more pronounced in *The Demi-Gods*, though, and it is significant that the later text includes no mention of the city, for cities are places of boundaries and suffocation in Stephens' philosophy. Indeed, the few towns and villages that are briefly glimpsed in this novel are described as places that are 'compact of ugliness and stupidity'.[39]

It is also significant that *The Demi-Gods* includes no mention of the police, for this reinforces the idea that Travellers inhabit a world that is beyond the pale of 'organized society'. It also avoids the presence of a body of characters who were despised by Stephens. In many of his stories, the police are associated with brutality and self-interest, and they are considered the upholders of colonialism, capitalism and an unjust system of law. Stephens' opinion of the police was perhaps most explicitly stated in *The Insurrection in Dublin*, when he recalled the 'unparalleled savagery' with which the police force treated the workers during the Lockout. Irish people 'fear the police', he commented, 'and they have very good reason to do so'.[40] Without the inhibiting presence of either the police force or the city, it seems entirely appropriate to read *The Demi-Gods* as a manifestation of the Dionysian principle.

However, Martin's reference to Dionysius is also interesting insofar as each of the three 'celebrated' characteristics – passion, imagination, excess – finds expression in the history of the stereotype of the Traveller. It is certainly the case that Stephens drew upon a received lore about Travellers in his depiction of Eileen, Patsy and Mary, and each of his characters embodies many of the defining features of the established type. Each of his Travellers is quick to temper, for example, and each of them speaks with ferocity, licence and abandon. Patsy bears many similarities with the traditional stereotypical image of the Traveller man (he is a wily thief who appears both servile and domineering, for instance), and Eileen and Mary are both ascribed a range of characteristics which accord with standard images of the female 'tinker'. Eileen is portrayed as a feisty figure with lapsed morals and a fondness for drink, while Mary is more reserved in manner but is granted an innate sensuality, signified through the prolonged references to her body and hair. At times these descriptions border on the voyeuristic – at one stage, for instance, the narrator fantasises that 'under [Mary's] clumsy garments one divined a body to be

---

[39] Stephens, *Demi-Gods*, p. 51
[40] Stephens, *Insurrection in Dublin*, pp 45, 64

adored as a revelation' – and this fits into the predominantly male tradition of eroticising female Travellers in literature.[41]

Travellers are also depicted in the conventional guise of 'children of nature' in *The Demi-Gods*, and are said to be able to read seasonal rhythms and weather patterns to a heightened degree. They are also shown to inhabit a space which is peripheral and unfamiliar ('with [settled] people … they had scarcely anything to say, and the housefolk looked on the strollers with a suspicion which was almost a fear'),[42] and their world is primed with a volatile charge which distinguishes it from the safer and more mundane – or Apollonian – concerns of bourgeois Ireland.[43] 'Sometimes [the angels and the Mac Canns] came on gatherings of tinkers and pedlars, tramps and trick-men', the narrator remarks, 'and in the midst of these they would journey towards a fair. Uproarious nights then! Wild throats yelling at the stars and much loud trampling on the roads as the women fought and screeched, and the men howled criticism and encouragement, and came by mere criticism themselves to battle'.[44]

Such instances of spontaneous violence are obviously indebted to a tradition of type and are characteristic of Stephens' engagement with Travellers in this text. They also find expression in some of his other prose narratives. In *The Charwoman's Daughter*, for instance, the narrator alludes to the 'wonderful tales of great fights and cunning tricks' that the worldly policeman tells the innocent Mary – wonderful tales 'of men and women whose whole lives were tricks, of people who did not know how to live except by theft and violence; people who were born by stealth, who ate by subterfuge, drank by dodges, got married in attics, and slid into death by strange, subterranean passages'.[45] Significantly, the policeman's collection of wonderful tales includes the intriguingly entitled – but unfortunately undeveloped – 'stories of The Eight Tinkers'. Moreover, elsewhere in the same text, the briefest of references to an imaginary Traveller forms part of a series of explosive images, which include 'a dynamite cartridge, a drunken tinker, [and] a mad dog', and these images are used by the narrator to suggest anything which is 'unexpected' or haphazard in life.[46] It is this sense of 'wonder' and the unexpected which lies at the heart of

---

[41] Stephens, *Demi-Gods*, pp 55-56
[42] Ibid., p. 52
[43] *Oxford Dictionary*, p. 72. According to the *Oxford Dictionary*, once again, Apollonian relates to the god Apollo and also 'to the rational, ordered and self-disciplined aspects of human nature. Compare with Dionysiac', it suggests.
[44] Stephens, *Demi-Gods*, p. 143
[45] Stephens, *Charwoman's Daughter*, p. 50
[46] Ibid., p. 122

Stephens' references to 'tinkers' in *The Charwoman's Daughter*, and it is also central to his representation of Travellers in *The Crock of Gold*.

In *The Crock of Gold*, the Philosopher happens upon a group of Travellers while he is on his journey to the Celtic god, Angus Óg. This group comprises a comic love triangle of two men and one woman, and each of these characters remains unnamed for the duration of their brief cameo. The Travellers are boldly sketched by Stephens and exhibit many of the defining characteristics of the traditional type. They are heard before they are seen, for instance, and their speech is described as 'loud and fierce'. Moreover, their passions are quickly roused and the Traveller woman, in particular, appears as a rather dissolute character. They fight among themselves, threaten those that they meet (including the Philosopher), and show great cruelty towards their donkey. They even inhabit a familiar location, as they are found on 'a small, narrow road', which is an offshoot of the substantial path along which the Philosopher – and the text – has been travelling.[47] With each of these points in mind it is interesting to note that some critics have claimed to discern a familiar intertextual quality to their presence in *The Crock of Gold*. 'The tinkers are refugees from Synge', Martin has argued, 'problematically involved with a social institution alien to their freebooting way of life'.[48]

Comments on intertextuality and literary repetition are pertinent (although one might ask why limit them to Synge's *The Tinker's Wedding* when Travellers were so prominent in other key texts of the Literary Revival), as are discussions about the 'tinkers' problematic engagement with the world around them. Such comments only realize part of the Travellers' full signifying potential, however, for in *The Crock of Gold* they also offer a perspective on the world that is new to the Philosopher, and this is what makes them critically important for Stephens' narrative. From the moment that they appear, the Travellers contest what seems to be obvious to the Philosopher – when he explains to them that he is on his way to see Angus Óg, they respond by asking him 'How do you know he wants to see you?'[49] This sets the tone for the rest of their conversation, as the 'tinkers' and the Philosopher struggle to comprehend one another. The entire episode, which runs to less than a dozen pages, is punctuated by questions, confusions and misunderstandings, and the only thing that is clear is that they are talking at cross-purposes. They have divergent opinions when it comes to a wide range of subjects (such as marriage, knowledge and suitable topics for

---

[47] Stephens, *Crock of Gold*, p. 91
[48] Martin, *James Stephens*, p. 48
[49] Stephens, *Crock of Gold*, p. 93

great arguments), and they disagree when they attempt to define what constitutes 'wisdom'.

For the Philosopher, wisdom is abstract and cerebral, whereas for the Traveller woman it is something that enables her to scavenge for food and to survive on the road. 'Isn't it wisdom to go through the world without fear', she asks the Philosopher, 'and not to be hungry in a hungry hour?'[50] Her words prompt the Philosopher to revise his opinion, and it is worth noting that it is during his time with the Travellers that he experiences sensations which enable him to move beyond the world of thought. In a moment of impulse, the Traveller woman breaks off her relationship with her companions and decides to marry the Philosopher. She ignores the latters' objections that he is already married ('Don't be making any argument with me now', she warns him, 'for I won't stand it'), and defends him against the threats of the spurned rivals. As she draws close to him, the narrator notes:

> There was a flutter at his heart which was terrifying, but not unpleasant. Quickening through his apprehension was an expectancy which stirred his pulses into speed. So rapidly did his blood flow, so quickly were a hundred impressions visualized and recorded, so violent was the surface movement of his brain that he did not realise he was unable to think and that he was only seeing and feeling.[51]

This is a new experience for the Philosopher, and in the context of the larger narrative it is one of several lessons that he and his wife must learn if they are to achieve the quasi-Blakean state of a 'matrimony of minds' which is the novel's final goal.[52] However, in this context it could be argued that it is significant that it is the Traveller woman who educates the Philosopher in the ways of the body, for this accords with a standard belief that all Travellers can be defined by their physicality – and Traveller women, in particular, by their sensuality and erotic ease. It is also significant that the sensations that are aroused in the Philosopher are unexpected – they are 'violent', disorienting ('he did not realize ...') and 'terrifying', and they open up new insights into the world.

It is this sense of new insights which ultimately defines Stephens' use of the Traveller figure in literature. Traveller characters offer unorthodox perspectives with which to examine – and critique – received assumptions and dominant prejudices. They enable Stephens to explore relations and concerns which might otherwise be constituted as common sense (such as attitudes towards labour,

---

[50] Ibid., p. 99
[51] Ibid., pp 97-98
[52] Ibid., p. 120

theft, property and possession), and they give voice to his fundamental belief that these relations are degrading and biased. According to the cultural theorist Errol Lawrence, complex ideological strategies underlie the claim that anything should be 'taken for granted' or considered 'common sense'. Far from being obvious or natural, Lawrence has remarked that such appeals are always informed by structures of power, and that they always 'act at one and the same time to foreclose any discussion about certain ideas and practices and to legitimate them'.[53] In other words, appeals for common sense authorize assertions of interest and naturalize forms of discrimination and injustice.

By using Traveller characters to disrupt his reader's preconceptions about such themes as property, labour and theft, and by granting those characters a privileged perspective in his texts, it could be argued that Stephens' work is challenging and subversive. It is certainly the case that some critics have interpreted his work in this light. Augustine Martin has remarked that Stephen's novels are 'always radical and frequently subversive', for example, while John Wilson Foster has commented on the 'spiritual socialism' and 'democratic vision' at the heart of this writer's work.[54] It could also be argued that Stephens' Travellers are 'subversive' because they provide the means for a necessary release from an otherwise stultified world – they speak with a certain licence, after all, and they refuse to obey the laws and inhibitions of those around them. To cite but one instance, in *The Demi-Gods* the slightest of references to a band of 'hairy tinkers ... who marched in the angriest of battalions and who spoke a language composed entirely of curses' hints at a radical subaltern presence in Ireland, and offers the possibility of a radically energized and critically uncensored voice.[55] The danger, however, is that such references can also be taken to conform to many settled readers' expectations about Travellers and to accord with the received 'wisdom' of the traditional type.

Despite – or because of – the radical potential of his textual representations, it is worth asking whether Stephens ultimately – and perhaps unwittingly – re-inscribes his Traveller characters within a tradition of type. It is interesting that the narrator of *The Demi-Gods* is of the opinion that Patsy was 'very mobile' in one field or direction only ('all his freedom lay in one direction', the narrator remarks, 'and outside of that pasturage he could never go'); it is also telling that

---

[53] Errol Lawrence, 'Just plain common sense: the "roots" of racism', in Centre for Contemporary Cultural Studies (ed.) *The Empire strikes back: race and racism in 70's Britain* (London, 1982), p. 48
[54] Martin, *James Stephens*, p. 61; Foster, *Fictions of the literary revival*, pp 271, 248
[55] Stephens, *Demi-Gods*, p. 53

Patsy is considered part of a 'gigantic underworld' in which he is said to move 'with almost absolute freedom'.[56] The qualifying words in both statements are worth stressing – '*one*', '*almost*' – and suggest that references to subversion and freedom need to be interpreted cautiously in this book. Such words denote the existence of dominant structures of power (notwithstanding the absence of the law and the police force in this text), and intimate the very real restrictions which are placed on the Mac Canns' movements in the world of the novel. It is worth asking, however, whether these restrictions also translate, in a textual sense, into the representative strategies which are available to Stephens in his design of *The Demi-Gods*.

Some might argue that this argument is ambiguous, insofar as Stephens is said to have subverted and yet to have been simultaneously restricted by the demands of an established form or type. However, it is worth bearing in mind that such ambiguities are consistent with Stephens' larger use of contradiction and counterpoint. This ambiguity might also be explained by way of Elizabeth Butler Cullingford's shrewd observation that 'the dividing line between a repressive stereotype and an empowering symbol of identity is often very narrow'.[57] Cullingford's observation, though, should be supplemented with an acknowledgement that such ambiguities are also expressive of the dangers which are implicit in any engagement with an established tradition of type. An attempt to deconstruct a received way of thinking often runs the risk of re-presenting that way of thinking in a resuscitated or familiar form. Part of Stephens' importance, to my mind, is that his work bears the trace of this ambiguity, as he strove to transcend received opinions (by granting Travellers a privileged perspective and providing portraits which are sensitive and challenging) only to remain attracted to familiar preconceptions and traditional types (the reference to the 'hairy tinkers ... who spoke a language ... of curses' being a case in point). All of which is to say that Stephens' work bears witness to the difficulties of responding to – or writing outside of, or against – an established discursive system, and for this reason he is vital to any critical discussion about Travellers and settled strategies of literary representation.

---

[56] Ibid., pp 46-7
[57] Elizabeth Butler Cullingford, *Gender and history in Yeats' love poetry* (Cambridge, 1993), p. 37

CHAPTER FIVE

HISTORY AS DIALOGUE:
AN ANTHROPOLOGICAL PERSPECTIVE

SINÉAD NÍ SHÚINÉAR[1]

In the early 1950s the Irish Folklore Commission carried out the only systematic survey relating to Travellers ever undertaken in this country, in the form of a 'tinker questionnaire' distributed to volunteer contributors (many of them schoolmasters) asking both what they knew, and what was locally believed, regarding Traveller names, trades, movements, origins and so on. The replies comprise an extremely valuable source of information which is only now, half a century on, being systematically analysed. However – title notwithstanding – the questionnaire does not tell us about Travelling People. It is a survey of non-Travellers: their perceptions, beliefs, and attitudes. Indeed there was no suggestion that Travellers be approached and questioned directly, despite the questionnaire being distributed two decades after An Máistir Pádraig Mac Gréine[2] had gone into deepest, darkest roadside Ireland, sat around fires chatting with people, and lived to tell the tale.[3] The notion that information should be gathered, not from members of the group, but from admittedly hostile non-members with little or no direct contact save of the most superficial,

---

[1] The author gratefully acknowledges the assistance of an Irish Research Council for the Humanities and Social Sciences Post-Doctoral Fellowship in conjunction with Trinity College, Dublin, under which much of the research outlined in this paper was carried out.
[2] '*Máistir*', literally 'Master' in Irish Gaelic, was the standard title for male primary school teachers in Ireland at the time. In Mac Gréine's case, however, it has solidified into an affectionate and respectful nickname, 'the' Master, due to his continuing involvement well into his 100s. The 75th anniversary edition of *Béaloideas. Iris an Chumainn le Bealoideas Éireann. The Journal of the Folklore of Ireland Society*, 69/2001, is dedicated to him and features a photograph of him on its cover.
[3] Pádraig Mac Gréine, 'Irish Tinkers or "Travellers"', in *Béaloideas,* 3 (1931), pp 170-86; Mac Gréine, 'Further Notes on Tinkers' "Cant"', in *Béaloideas,* 3 (1932), pp 290-303; Mac Gréine, 'Some Notes on Tinkers and their "Cant"', in *Béaloideas,* 4 (1934) pp 259-63.

functional type, is remarkable, but no one found it so. That in itself reveals a great deal about the relations between our peoples.

Equally significant is the fact that this initiative came under the auspices of the Folklore Commission. History is, by popular ethnocentric definition, based on written records; 'pre-history' is, after all, synonymous with 'pre-writing'. By this reckoning, those who do not keep written records, have no history. Yes, there are non-literate peoples who keep strict accounts of the past – who could forget the scene in *Roots*, where author Alex Hailey tracks down a *seanchaí*[4] in the Gambia who confirms that Kunta Kinte did indeed disappear while in the forest looking for wood to make a drum?[5] That is one approach open to non-literate cultures and the one we, as literate people, are most comfortable with, because it is the closest to written history: a purportedly immutable official version created, held and transmitted by specialists (although, given current trends in revisionism and counter-revisionism, the notion of a single correct vision of the past is very much up for grabs). At the other end of the continuum, occupied by Gypsies and Travellers, lies a qualitatively different approach, without specialists or orthodoxy, in which the whole of a society owns a seamless continuum of past and present continually reinterpreted and reshaped in the telling. Not only is there no definitive version now, there is also no former definitive version with which to compare it, for good or ill.

Which bits of the past are deemed relevant enough to remember varies from culture to culture and indeed within a given culture over time. Back in the early 70s, as the Leaving Certificate[6] loomed, our history teacher announced that we hadn't enough time to cover both remaining chapters in the textbook, and would have to choose between Irish missionaries in Africa, and the industrial revolution. She opted for the missionaries, on the grounds that – and I quote – 'The industrial revolution wasn't important'. Earlier again, when I was in primary school, 'history' was pretty much synonymous with political and military facts: the battles, the kings. We memorised a lot of dates. By the time my own children started looking at, for example, the Romans, the focus was on clothing, architecture, religion – how they lived, which in my time did not even count as history. My teachers of decades ago would search in vain for 'history' in today's school 'history' books. I point this out in order to impress upon the reader that a shifting vision of the past and its relevance is not a characteristic

---

[4] *Seanchaí*: a bearer of oral tradition [Irish Gaelic]. I apply this term from European experience to an African analogue in order to highlight cultural overlap and thus de-exoticise both.
[5] Alex Haley, *Roots* (London, 1991), p. 679.
[6] Leaving Certificate: the Irish state examination terminating second-level schooling.

unique to exotic others who do not record that past in writing, but endemic to human experience, including that of Irish non-Travellers.

Dissensus regarding the past is, however, particularly pronounced in cross-cultural situations, including the Traveller/non-Traveller interface. The most important mental adjustment the researcher into another culture's history has to make, is to grasp that she has no idea what she will find there; the details she deems crucial may be lacking altogether, while she finds herself inundated in 'irrelevant' data. Irrelevant to whom? Not to the people who are passing them on, obviously. The fact that they choose the focus they do already tells you something, if you have the wit to listen. If you have not, you are just going to be frustrated by their 'failure' to cover issues you think are important and they do not.

Combining the above points – the universal truth that people choose to remember what they find relevant about their own past, and that non-literate cultures have the option of reinterpreting that past without fear of contradiction – we come to the Great Impasse, the perennial question, 'How do Travellers themselves explain their origins?' This is doubly ethnocentric: it assumes both a focus, and a consensus, that simply do not exist. The truth is that most Travellers do not think about their origins nearly as much as non-Travellers do, and that those who do think about the issue come up with theories that make sense to them, constructed out of whatever information they have been exposed to, both internal – discussions with other Travellers, stories they have overheard – and external, especially coverage in the mass media. Different people come up with different arguments but no one has the last word.

The following verbatim extract from an interview with a sixty-year-old man gives an indication of the sort of theorising one can get from Travellers who have devoted some thought to the topic of origins:

> The Travellers are almost, nearly almost, the same time as Our Lord. Not too – maybe seventy or eighty year behind that. But they're not too far away from it. The Traveller built their own little mud-walled houses, and they had little bits of land, things like that. And they were always on the road. Definitely on the road. The first Travelling man did start from the road, did really start on the road. He was never in a house. Now, that is the truth, because I know that from me grandfather's side, he often told me about it, that the Traveller never was in a house. But he says, in my time, now, he says, in me father's time, my father, he says – that was my great-grandfather – built, he says, a place, a house, on a half acre, around that time. There was people, English people, called the sheriffs, they took over that little – same as this garden here! The farmer takes it over, runs me out to the road! And he's bulldozed this, and run this piece of ground in with his own land. And that left the Travellers on the road.

Summarising this overview of Traveller history: Travellers have been simultaneously exclusively nomadic, and exclusively sedentary, since the first century BCE, but only took to the roads when evicted by English sheriffs in the speaker's great-grandfather's time (the mid-19th century). Similarly, on the subject of language, this individual told me that up to 'the time of the Tans – back in the Tans' time, Troubles time', Travellers had no language of their own, 'only the Irish, that we're speaking now'.[7] But we were speaking English, not Irish, and 'the time of the Tans' was the 1920s, decades after the Gypsilorists compiled their 'Shelta' wordlists inter alia in the slums of Liverpool.[8]

Such narrative is frustrating, if taken at face value: it is full of internal contradictions and flies in the face of documented fact. It is not 'history' as understood by academia; Travellers simply have no such thing, and searching for a shared, immutable, linear, verifiable Traveller vision of their own past is ethnocentric folly. If, on the other hand, we accept such accounts as legend, or myth, we begin to appreciate their value at a deeper level, not least in what they tell us of Traveller attitudes towards the past itself, where the Time of Our Lord and the Time of the Tans coexist and blur.

This is not a paper about anybody's version of 'where Travellers come from'. Indeed it addresses none of the burning questions of Traveller history as defined by non-Travellers. I make no apology for this: I am, after all, not an historian, but an anthropologist. My discipline overlaps with history[9]; indeed I was struck, on going through my unpublished papers for inclusion on the University of

---

[7] The Black and Tan were created as a paramilitary adjunct to the Royal Irish Constabulary [police force] during the Anglo-Irish war (aka 'the Troubles'), 1920-1921, and achieved notoriety in popular memory.

[8] Canon J. Ffrench, 'Additional Notes on the Irish Tinkers and their language', in the *Journal of the Gypsy Lore Society (JGLS)* 2:2, (1890), pp 127-8; Charles G. Leland, 'Shelta, the Tinkers' Talk', in *New Quarterly Magazine*, 111, (1880), pp 136-41; Leland, 'Shelta', in *JGLS*, 2: 6, (1891), pp 321-3; Leland, 'Shelta, or The lost language of the Bards, and how it was recovered', in *JGLS*, 2: 11, (1907-8a), pp 73-6. Leland, 'The Tinkers', in *JGLS*, 2: 11, (1907-8b), pp 76-82. Leland, 'The Tinkers' Talk', in *JGLS*, 2: 1 (1907-8c), pp 168-80 (first published as "Shelta" chapter of *The Gypsies* 1881-2). Kuno Meyer, 1891 'On the Irish origin and age of Shelta' in *JGLS,* 2: 5, (1891), pp. 257-66; Meyer, 1909 'The secret languages of Ireland' in *JGLS,* 2 (1909), pp. 241-6. J. Sampson, 'Tinkers and their Talk', in *JGLS*, 2: 4, (1890), pp 204-21. Alick G. Wilson, 'Shelta – The Tinkers' Talk', in *JGLS*, 2: 2 (1890), pp 121-2.

[9] Or rather, most schools of anthropology, with the exception of those most prevalent in English-speaking countries, cultivate an historical perspective on the societies they study. For a critique of ahistoric ethnography, see Thomas A. Acton, 'Academic success and political failure: a review of modern social science writing in English on Gypsies', in *Ethnic and Racial Studies*, 2:2, (1979), pp 231-241.

Limerick Traveller History website http://www.history.ul.ie/heatravinit/, that all of them deal with history in one form or another. At the same time, the foci, sources and methods of these disciplines are very different, effectively mirror images of one another. While history analyses the past in order to cast light on the present, anthropology concerns itself with understanding the present (which is of course a product of the past) through observation and analysis of, current behaviour, cultural artefacts, and narrative; given that the cultures we focus on are often non-literate, history's prime source, the written word, may play little or no role. Historians now realise that the powerful individuals who have documented their economic, political, military etc. doings so thoroughly are only part of the story, and are now balancing this by seeking to reconstruct the day-to-day realities of 'ordinary people', women included. Anthropology, by contrast, has always focused on those excluded from the official picture, whether the 'natives' of colonised lands or 'folk' culture at home.[10] Given that these excluded peoples are in a vulnerable position vis à vis the society embodied by academia, it is imperative that the anthropologist's quest for truth not increase their vulnerability, and the discipline has evolved a number of what one researcher calls 'disutilisation strategies' to protect the individuals who make the leap of faith required to open up and talk to us.[11] It is the desire to protect such individuals, rather than (as sometimes assumed) a wish to present anonymous voices as somehow embodying entire cultures, that lies behind the ethnographic convention of not identifying sources and indeed of obfuscating incidental details (age, number of children, placenames) which provide clues to that identity.

Anthropology overlaps with sociology, as well, in a number of obvious ways, but there are crucial differences, the most fundamental of which is scale. Sociology deals with hundreds, even thousands, in a relatively superficial way, pre-selecting representative informants through sampling and ensuring comparability of the information they provide through standardised questionnaires statistically analysed to blur detail into the big, e.g. national, picture. Anthropology, by contrast, typically deals with relatively small groups (a single village, neighbourhood or community) and in so doing seeks to produce intimate, sharply detailed descriptions including of contentious, and

---

[10] Broadly speaking, anthropology in countries (such as England and France) which had colonies, has focused on the indigenous peoples of those colonies, while countries (such as Sweden) which had none or (like Poland) were themselves colonised, have focused on their own folklore. Until recently, sociology alone dealt with urban groups and cultural elites within the 'developed' world; anthropology now sees these as appropriate areas of research and is turning its attentions towards them.

[11] R.M. Lee, *Dangerous Fieldwork* (London, 1995)

certainly of personal, topics. Questionnaires (as opposed to discrete questions) play no role here. Anthropological research, with its emphasis on seeing the world as others see it, is correctly a response to the realities and concerns of the researched rather than the imposition of one's own; it is interactive and idiosyncratic.

The overwhelming majority of my research is unstructured day-to-day interaction and observation, supplemented by formal interviewing. My initial doctoral research was carried out among friends, and people with whom they put me in touch: a dispersed but unbroken network. My post-doctoral research, by contrast, took as its starting point existing lists of Irish Traveller surnames [amalgamated in a paper available at on the UL http://www.history.ul.ie/heatravinit/ website], with the wildly ambitious aim of compiling an exhaustive list of Traveller surnames current on the island of Ireland, obtaining a family tree – and thus the kinship connections – for each of these surnames, and getting someone from each of them to talk to me about their family history. Pursuing this research entailed seeking out surnames that had not cropped up in other people's trees – people who do not know other Travellers I know, who might put in a good word for me. These strangers had to be located through non-Traveller middlemen, who presented my case for me; I had no control over how these individuals get on with the people they approached on my behalf, or how they explained what I was trying to do, but those unknowables influenced how people perceived me, in addition to my being a non-Traveller, and a researcher. When I finally did sit down to talk, it was therefore with a great deal of invisible baggage attached. Under the circumstances, it was remarkable just how much people were willing to share with me; families are, after all, the most emotional topic in the world, and doing family trees means bringing up memories of loved ones now dead, of people with whom one has quarrelled, occasionally even of desertions and other scandals.

It is crucial that people be heard in the first person; it is equally crucial that their identities be protected without being falsified. If I were to label individuals quoted, even with a number, it would still be possible, by piecing together all of a given speaker's quotes, to identify them. Similarly, putting dates on the interviews, many of which were carried out at training centres/development groups, would effectively identify where they took place and thus who spoke to me on the day. Instead, in this and all my work I reproduce quotes with no indication of who said them so that no one – in most cases not even the speakers themselves – can be certain who said what. It is precisely because these are individuals with distinct voices and strong personalities that I have to go to such lengths to protect them. What I am aiming for is deniability – the reader may think they know who said what, but they cannot prove it. Lest this seem paranoid, bear in mind Grönfors' observation that keeping Gypsies' identity secret from non-Gypsies is a lot easier than keeping it secret from other Gypsies.[12] Traveller friends are regular visitors to my home, and frequently ask to see my photo albums; they also chat with me, and see me chatting with others, in the local shops.[13] In other words, any Traveller I know can easily figure out which other Travellers I am in touch with. Given that much of the information revealed is of a highly sensitive nature, and indeed that telling non-Travellers anything whatever may be interpreted as a form of betrayal, failure to protect speakers' anonymity could have direct negative consequences that would be a poor way of repaying their trust.

A total of 23,681 individuals self-identified as Traveller in the last [2002] national census, making them approximately one half of one percent of the total population.[14] They are, to put it mildly, outnumbered, but, unlike Ireland's equally outnumbered religious minorities, have virtually no presence in political or professional circles where decision-making occurs. When it comes to Traveller-related issues, decision-makers are very much in tune with the attitudes of society in general: it remains acceptable, both here and – as we saw most recently during the 2005 election campaign – in Britain[15], to say things about Travellers one would not dream of saying in relation to any other group; as recently as 1999 the Mayo county councillor who recommended all Travellers be electronically tagged was acquitted of incitement to hatred.[16]

The bottom line is that a tiny, powerless minority dispersed among an openly hostile majority must, if it is to survive, placate rather than provoke that majority. This tactic is pursued at every level, including one-to-one encounters. Real dialogue, in which people communicate as equals, with the freedom to disagree and contradict, is structurally precluded from the formal interview in which each participant is an embodiment of a power differential. The researcher – no matter how well intentioned, or indeed malicious or incompetent, she may be – is looking for information, much of which is essential to the Traveller's protection; this is most obvious in relation to language issues, but applies across

---

[12] Martti Grönfors, *Blood Feuding Among Finnish Gypsies*, (Helsinki, 1978, 3rd edition), p. 184.
[13] I have, since 1981, lived in Clondalkin, a Dublin suburb with one of the country's highest concentrations of Travellers.
[14] Information from Central Statistics Office website. For full statistical data on Irish Travellers, go to www.cso.ie/census/Vol8.htm (accessed 15 August, 2006). Information from the 2006 census will not be available until 2007.
[15] See *Sunday Times*, 20, March 2005; *Guardian*, 21 March 2005.
[16] For coverage, see all Irish national newspapers, 02/03/99.

the board. Both sides know that the researcher will – accurately or otherwise – convey whatever information they acquire to other non-Travellers, whose subsequent view of, and decisions relating to, Travellers will be influenced by it. The researcher has the luxury of being able to ignore or even deny this power differential, because she has nothing to lose by so doing; the Traveller cannot afford to forget it for a moment, no matter how much she may like the researcher as an individual.

This means that non-Traveller research among Travellers is a particularly fraught type of intercultural dialogue in which both sides promote their own, mostly incompatible, interests: the researcher wants 'the truth', while the Traveller wants above all to placate the researcher. Classically, this is achieved by confirming the researcher's existing notions (where these are negative, they will be assigned to other, unrelated families); where the researcher appears to have few preconceptions, the speaker is free to fill in the blanks with whatever she feels will best satisfy the researcher's needs, including pure invention. A more subtle tactic is to use every question as a sort of springboard for rambling anecdotes of little relevance, giving the impression of conveying vast amounts of data. In either case, the end result is that the researcher goes away happy, unaware that they have acquired exactly that information the Traveller wished to convey.

Italian anthropologist Leonardo Piasere, who pursued research similar to mine, describes his culture shock on visiting his uncle, a farmer, after months of immersion in Roma society. He was forcibly struck by the contrast in conversation topics: farmers talk about crops, the weather, and EU directives, but not about the central topic of Roma conversation, namely, who is marrying whom and how they are linked; Roma, for their part, do not discuss agriculture. This seemingly banal observation is in fact a revelation of profound truth: people talk about what is important to them (and do not talk about what is not).[17] The anthropologist must be attuned to this, and adjust her focus accordingly, rather than attempt to impose her own, equally arbitrary, interests on the people she wishes to understand. In the case of Irish Travellers, 'history' in the culture-free sense of 'how the past is felt to shape the present', is synonymous with kinship.

Coser makes the crucially important point that as urban industrial society has undermined kinship it has created voluntary associations (sports clubs, trade

---

[17] Leonardo Piasere, *Máre Roma. Catégories humaines et structure sociale. Une contribution à l'ethnologie tsigane* (Paris, 1985), pp 174-5. Sinéad Ní Shúinéar, 'Irish Travellers: ethnolect, alliance, control', (Unpublished PhD, University of Greenwich, 2003).

unions, charitable bodies ...) to replace it, forgetting that these are innovative substitutions, and assuming that without them there is 'no' order.[18] Kinship is seen as archaic when it is seen at all, and has been used by outside observers to 'other' the Irish, though usually only in terms of its allegedly anachronistic intensity: Evans, listing Ireland's many 'prehistoric' characteristics, tells us that 'First in importance is the strength of blood-ties in extended family groups ...'.[19] The *Report of the Commission on Itinerancy* denied Traveller ethnicity on the grounds that 'There is no system of unified control, authority or government and no individual or group of individuals has any powers or control over the itinerant members of the community' – followed by six paragraphs of observations on their intense kin ties[20] and the observation that 'Ties of kinship, even the most removed type, are strong, and bearing in mind the extent of inter-marriage the numbers related in this way must be considerable'.[21]

All observers agree that kinship – a by-product of marriage – forms the armature of Irish Traveller social organisation. McCarthy focused on marriage *senso stricto,* with vague generalisations about 'tribes'.[22] The first detailed, largely fanciful, coverage of this topic was undertaken by Barnes, followed by George Gmelch's *The Urbanization of an Itinerant People* [originally published 1977], the first examination of Irish Traveller culture by a trained anthropologist.[23] Unfortunately, the atypically sociopathic population among whom he did his research [see "Half Travellers", http://www.history.ul.ie/heatravinit/] led him to the unique conclusion that Traveller society is 'atomistic ... a highly individualistic environment ... the nuclear family represents the major structural unit ...'[24] contradicted by his assertion that strangers start off by 'reconstructing ... family history ... When a common relative was discovered, social relations between the individuals were suddenly on much firmer

---

[18] Lewis A. Coser, *The Functions of Social Conflict* (London, 1968, originally published 1956), p. 141
[19] E. Estyn Evans, *Irish Folk Ways* (London, 1957), p. 10.
[20] *Report of the Commission on Itinerancy* (Dublin, 1963), pp 37-9.
[21] Ibid., p. 87.
[22] Patricia McCarthy, 'Itinerancy and poverty: a study in the sub-culture of poverty', (M A Thesis, University College Dublin, 1971), pp 43, 82.
[23] Bettina Barnes, 'Irish Travelling People' in F. Rehfisch (ed.) *Gypsies, Tinkers and Other Travellers* (London, 1975) pp 231-56. George Gmelch, *The Irish Tinkers: the urbanization of an itinerant people.* (Prospect Heights, 1985)
[24] G. Gmelch, *The Irish Tinkers,* pp 91-2.

ground'.[25] Helleiner, like her predecessors, is mostly concerned with marriage, dealing with kinship in the practical contexts of mobility and residence.[26]

Many commentators on 'Gypsies' note that, insofar as they use surnames, these are a meaningless sop of conformity to the demands of Gadjo [non-Gypsy] bureaucracy.[27] My doctoral research revealed that this does not apply to Irish Travellers, who habitually identify their own, and others', groups by surname. Individuals may assume pseudonyms as a protective measure, but internally there is no confusion as to 'real' surname – or surnames, since different links, traced equally through both parents (maternal links are just as 'real' as paternal) are stressed in different contexts.

Having identified the importance of these ties to the people in question, they became the focus of my research. Note that drawing up Traveller family trees is not, in itself, innovative, but doing so in collaboration is unprecedented; like Gmelch, Helleiner concealed the fact that she was compiling family trees from those concerned.[28] In pursuing them, I did not ask about abstractions such as terminology, roles or rules (these come out between the lines, and in behaviour). Instead, I asked about parents, siblings and spouses as far up and down stream as they could go. Then – since my focus was alliance through marriage – I eliminated all unmarried individuals except those who (due to advanced age) were labelled unmarriageable. I then drew up the information, brought it back and ran it by the person again. It took at least two, and sometimes up to five, sessions before they were satisfied that the diagrams were as accurate, and as detailed, as we could get them, at which point I handed them a full set; people were genuinely pleased with them because they look well, and, being colour-coded, can be 'read' even by non-literate individuals.[29] Note that, unlike the

---

[25] Ibid., p. 96.

[26] See for example, Jane Helleiner, 'The Tinker's Wedding revisited: Irish Traveller marriage' in M. Salo (ed.), *100 Years of Gypsy Studies* (The Gypsy Lore Society, Cheverly 1990), pp 77-85. Helleiner, *Irish Travellers: Racism and the politics of culture* (Toronto, 2000), pp 110-14, 126-7, 178-81.

[27] Ronald Lee, 'The Rom-Vlax Gypsies and the Kris-Romani' in *The American Journal of Comparative Law*, 45: 2 (1997), pp. 345-92; Judith Okely, *The Traveller-Gypsies*, (Cambridge, 1983), p. 175; Michael Stewart, *The time of the Gypsies* (Boulder, 1997), pp. 59-60; Ann Sutherland, 'Complexities of US Law and Gypsy identity' in *The American Journal of Comparative Law*, 45: 2, (1997), pp. 395-405.

[28] G. Gmelch, *The Irish Tinkers,* pp. 193-4. Helleiner, *Irish Travellers,* p.213.

[29] Unfortunately, being colour-coded, they are also prohibitively expensive to print, and so cannot be reproduced here; in time, however, I am hoping to make sample diagrams, and indeed all the findings of my IRCHSS-funded research, available online under the auspices of the Traveller Initiative of the History Department at the University of Limerick.

versions I give back to people, those for public display use pseudonyms: surnames are rendered as colours and first names replaced with random – not equivalent – Irish ones.

Although there are literally hundreds of Traveller surnames, diagrams typically have only one or two dominant ones; even the most comprehensive, with dozens of marriages, rarely have more than half a dozen, whether or not the individuals concerned are known to be blood related. In fact people often insist that named individuals who bear the same surname, and have intermarried, represent completely separate families. The most visually striking thing about my diagrams, then, is the very limited number of colours/surnames in each.

The second most striking thing about them, is that each colour/ surname is consistently associated with the same other colours/ surnames: the Blues, Greens and Yellows marry each other, but not the Browns, Reds and Oranges, who marry amongst themselves, and so on. Surnames do not intermarry indiscriminately, but within finite clusters, and have done so for generations.

The third most striking feature is the correlation between surname clusters and (known) ties between spouses. When people are listing their relatives and who they, and their children, are married to, I ask them to tell me any connections they are aware of, and my diagrams include all of them: these can be as straightforward as marriage between two siblings' children (first cousins), or as complex as siblings marrying spouses who are distantly blood related to each other, but not to them. As noted above, all intermarrying clusters comprise a mere handful of surnames, but there are dramatic differences between the types of links within them; on some of my diagrams, every individual is linked to every other in a variety of different ways, while others show marriages between apparently unlinked individuals, yet always within a finite cluster of surnames. Talking to people about their relatives, it becomes clear that some family groups consciously eschew consanguineous unions while others favour them, and families pursuing such different tactics do not normally intermarry. Marriage tactics in turn determine whether members of a given family are inclined to forget/downplay whatever links there are, or on the contrary to remember and even highlight them. For example, one family favouring tight intermarriage had me round for a family tree discussion that started about nine in the morning and was interrupted four hours later by an order to clear the table so we could eat, a break I sorely needed; I was dismayed, and enlightened, when conversation over dinner simply continued in the same (kinship) vein. This is what such families talk about: it matters. Their familiarity with their convoluted interconnectedness is, accordingly, encyclopaedic. By contrast, families who reject marriage between blood relations have relatively short collective memories concerning such undesirable links.

In the interview reproduced below, I encounter an unfamiliar surname and assume it was recently introduced by an in-marrying country man (i.e., a non-Traveller), whereas the person bearing it (from a family with a short collective memory) in fact has no idea how far back it goes. This illustrates the process of dialogue, including how I sometimes get things wrong and how, unless I know the person I am speaking with really well, they do not confront or correct me. I have since learnt that unusual surnames are by no means necessarily 'new' ones; surnames can – through a lack of sons to pass them on, emigration, and/or transformation [the process by which by which nicknames solidify into surnames – see below] decline. To place this in historical context, it is worth noting that only three of the eleven surnames most common among today's descendants of mid-19th century Irish Traveller emigrants to the US[30] are among the 132 on the most exhaustive, and up-to-date, list [31] compiled in Ireland[32], and only one of these 'American' surnames figures (in joint sixth place) on the Commission's list of the thirty-five most common.[33] Assigning geographical or temporal origins to Traveller surnames in the absence of in-family explanations is therefore speculative at best.

S[34] : What were you before you married?
O'White.
S: Really?! That's a completely new name to me! [both laugh] Are there many Travellers called O'White?
We're the only Travellers in Ireland, or England, called O'White. We're the only one family of O'Whites that there ever were. Now there's a population in the last, say, nine or ten years, there's five or six families of the O'Whites because we've our own children married and their children started up. So, there will be a big population of O'Whites after a while!

---

[30] M McDonagh and R McVeigh, *Minceir Neeja in the Thome Munkra: Irish Travellers in the USA* (Belfast, 1996), p. 37.
[31] Michael Flynn, 'Family Names of Travellers' (privately circulated, 2000).
[32] My data are currently being converted to electronic format by Mark Hanly, Department of Mathematics, NUI Maynooth.
[33] *Report of the Commission on Itinerancy,* Appendix XXXVIII.
[34] My contribution to dialogue is always preceded by 'S:' (for Sinéad). By including it, the process of gathering and interpreting information is rendered transparent. For discussion of dialogics in anthropology, see James Clifford, 'On Ethnographic Authority' in *The Predicament of Culture. Twentieth-Century Ethnography, Literature and Art* (anthology of texts by James Clifford, Boston, 1988), pp 21-54. , Vincent Crapanzano, 1980 *Tuhami, Portrait of a Moroccan* (Chicago, 1980), Kevin Dwyer, *Moroccan Dialogues: Anthropology in Question* (Baltimore, 1982), and D Tedlock, 'The analogical tradition and the emergence of a dialogical anthropology' in *Journal of anthropological research,* 35: 4 (1979), pp 387-400.

S: Please God! And do you know how the O'White family got started up? Was it with somebody marrying in?
Yeah, I would assume.
S: But you don't know. No family legends along those lines?
Yeah. As far as I can go back, that my grandfather, my *great*-grandfather, came from [placename], and my grandmother came from [placename]. She was an O'Red and he was a – No! I don't know what my great-grandmother's name was! My *own* grandmother was an O'Red married to an O'White.
S: On your father's side?
On my father's side. And on my mother's side, both my grandparents were Travelling People. My grandfather, Cathal O'Jade, came from [placename], and my grandmother, Tildín O'Maize ...
S: No. But on your father's side? Was the O'Whites country people?
I would assume that they'd come from ... Yes, yes.

A bearer of one of the Commission's top four surnames once remarked to me how tiresome she finds it that country people invariably greet her surname with, 'Oh! [Brown]! Do you know Mary [Brown] in [placename]?', comparing this to 'Oh! You're from London. You must know know my cousin John – he lives in London, too.' The group appears small and homogeneous from an outsider's perspective, but, seen from within, is vast and differentiated. Bearers of a given surname may or may not feel they have something in common with others who share that surname, but not the collective nickname; there may be no known blood or affinal ties, and relations may range from cordial to neutral or even hostile.

> **See, we are ['Flaherty'] McGreens. So the only way to distinguish when there's so many families, Sinéad, is, we are known as the ['Flaherty'] McGreens. So Daddy's father was never known as Brían McGreen, he used to be known as Brían ['Flaherty'], Old Brían ['Flaherty']. So even to this day now, if you were describing, trying to explain to another, strange Traveller who I am, I would always say I'm a ['Flaherty'] McGreen.**

In this instance[35], oral family history has a clear record of how this – and another – collective nickname was introduced:

> **Brían McGreen was married to a woman called Soineamha [Flaherty]. Not a McGreen.**
> *She was a genuine [Flaherty], like your surname, right?*
> **Now, there's thousands of the [Flahertys] today, right?**
> S: Yes.

---

[35] The following dialogue occurred between three speakers, differentiated by font.

And they all take their name from her. Because, to distinguish: she had a son called Tomás. Alright? And there was a number of Tomás McGreens camped at the camp. Everyone used to address her son, as Soineamha [Flaherty's] Tomás.³⁶ Hence the name, [Flaherty], stuck to him. So all his descendants –
S: Are the [Flahertys].
Because the name stuck. Now, he had a brother, right? A brother called Breandán McGreen. And the name they put on him was Breandán [Finnegan].
S: Why?
Just, Breandán [Finnegan]. Called him that.
S: Were there any [Finnegans] anywhere in the line?
No.
There is now, but they're not [Finnegans].
S: They just made it up.
Longford is full of [Finnegans].
But they're not [Finnegans], you understand me? I heard the song [Finnegan's Rainbow] was around that time.
S: How long ago are you talking about here? You're talking about great great grandparents.
You're just talking about after the Famine, at this stage.

Here a collective nickname is adopted via – but not directly from – an in-marrying non-Traveller woman's surname: one (and not, nota bene, all) of her sons takes it as an individual nickname, and his progeny bear it collectively. His brother gains an individual nickname from a entirely different source – a comical popular song – and it too is borne by his progeny.

Finnegan, like the name it replaces here, is a real surname with strongly localised (south) west of Ireland connotations but, in the Traveller context, exists solely as a collective nickname: today's 'Finnegans' may call themselves, and be known to others as, 'Finnegans', but Travellers know this is not their 'real' surname.

Note that in both cases, the collective nickname is a 'real' (non-Traveller) surname, unremarkable in the non-Traveller population. While Travellers themselves know that [Flahertys] and [Finnegans] are both 'really' McGreens, non-Travellers may draw no such distinction: one Garda assured me that the ['nicknames'] bore no relation to the [McGreys], when I knew from family

---

³⁶ Travellers habitually differentiate individuals by associating them with relatives – in this case, a man with his mother – but unlike the non-Traveller Irish do not do so in strict generational order, nor do these associations crystallise into formal nicknames, e.g. the eponymous hero of John B. Keane's *Dan Pheadai Aindi* (Dublin, 1977). *Dan Pheadai Aindi* translates as, Dan the son of Paddy the son of Andy.

histories that [McGrey] is their shared 'real' surname. This hints at how Traveller surnames may mutate over time: where a collective surname is unremarkable, it may be adopted or imposed as a 'real' surname, especially if collective identities have solidified as separate. Long-term geographical separation could be a factor (hence different surnames among Irish Travellers in Ireland and the United States) but such differentiation may occur without it.

Just how distinct the bearers of different collective nicknames sharing the same 'real' surname may be was brought home to me when I realised with a shock that McBlues who travelled from England to attend the trial of a McRed for the murder of their kinsman requested and received permission to set up camp for the duration beside McReds bearing a different collective nickname. The deadly animosity between the McBlues (or rather, these particular collective nickname McBlues) and one group of McReds did not extend to McReds who bear a different collective name.

I would add that these wheels within wheels greatly complicate the researcher's task, since it takes a long time to realise that e.g. the 'Finnegans' and the 'Flahertys' are both 'McGreens', and that the individual known as [Seán Finnegan] is also, *inter alia*, [Seán McGreen], ['Smiley' Finnegan] and ['Smiley' McGreen] (See Grönfors[37] re similar complications).

Given the crucial role played by clusters of intermarrying surnames, it seemed impossible that these collectivities not be formally labelled in some way, and I doggedly pursued the relevant terminology:

> S: Do words like 'clan' ever come into it? Do people use that word?
> **Not so much *within* Travellers. Outside Travellers, you hear it a lot.**
> S: As you know, the word *clann* is only the Irish word for 'family'.[38] You know that. So I thought it might be used.
> **No. It's not used, no. You see, when you're talking about Travellers, you don't distinguish them geographically, in one sense. You don't distinguish them work-wise. You distinguish them name-wise. So, you've groupings of names together, more so than ... Like, it's like saying, 'They're the Cheekies'. Immediately you're talking about *people*.**

---

[37] Martti Grönfors, 'Finnish Gypsies and the Police: An Examination of a Racial Minority and its Relationship with Law Enforcement Agents' (PhD thesis, London School of Economics, 1979), p. 257.
[38] The term 'clan' is broadly familiar to Anglophones from a Scots context where it describes a specific sociohistorical kinship system, here erroneously applied to an Irish context. A more accurate translation of the Irish homonym *clann* would be 'offspring' or, in a broader perspective, progeny; see Robin Fox, *The Tory Islanders: a people of the Celtic fringe* (Boston, 1978), p.69.

Here the speaker explicitly denies the relevance of geography 'in one sense' – i.e. that of 'where you live'. The collective nickname is the crucial group demarcator – and it can be geographical in the sense of associating people, not with where they live, but with where they go for burial when they die.[39]

Continuing our conversation:

> S: What words do you use to describe these different subdivisions? All of the [McBeiges] comprise a ...?
> **Number, not just one, but a number, of extended families.**
> S: Is that what you would call them normally, or is that what you call them because you're talking to me?
> **Country people ... It's because I'm talking to – If I was talking to anyone else, we would refer to them as 'one of the Gumbies', 'one of the Foxes', 'one of the Quinns' ...**
> S: Is there a term that people use ...?
> **That's the term.**
> S: You just would call them by name. You don't have ...
> **You would distinguish them by who – like, you'd say, if I was referring to some of the families from the north, I would say, you know, 'the Lindseys'. And people would then know, exactly who you were talking about.**
> S: I just want to know is there a word that describes ... the Lindseys are a ...?
> **There is, insofar as that there are a number of family groupings together ...**
> S: Would people use the word, 'family grouping'?
> **No! But that's what they are, if I'm talking to *you*.**
> S: I'm just wondering if there's a term for it. But there isn't, obviously.
> **You would refer to them as – say if he had a cousin, and even if they were kind of like, out, far-out cousins – he would refer to them as 'friends'. 'Friends of my own', or, meaning that they're cousins of my own, they're friends of my own.**

In other words, notwithstanding my repetition of senseless questions, Travellers themselves have no abstract label for any of these subdivisions; they are all simply *friends* – blood relations – of each other, and possibly also of the person referring to them.[40] Travellers do, occasionally, use terms such as 'clan' and

---

[39] Noted and characteristically interpreted by Sharon Bohn Gmelch, *Tinkers and Travellers Ireland's nomads*, (Dublin, 1975) p. 82, as 'Travellers are buried in the family's home county, often in the town from which their relations first went on the road.'

[40] Virtually every commentator on the non-Traveller Irish draws attention to their use of 'friend' as a synonym for 'blood relation' Hugh Brody, *Inishkillane. Change and Decline in the West of Ireland* (Harmondsworth, 1973), p. 132; E. Estyn Evans, *Irish folk ways*, p. 10; Evans, 'Peasant Beliefs in 19th-century Ireland' in D. J. Casey and R. E. Rhodes (eds.) *Views of the Irish peasantry 1800-1916* (Connecticut, 1977) p.39; John Messenger,

'tribe' that make sense to country people – but only when endeavouring to communicate with country people, *pace* Gmelch, Helleiner (who two pages later quotes a Traveller using the outdated PC neologism 'itinerant') and McCarthy.[41] In this as in so many other aspects of trying to make sense of Traveller realities, the researcher's ethnocentric expectations of what 'must' be there are either frustrated, or consciously humoured.

Another remarkable feature of my family tree diagrams is that first names are every bit as repetitive as surnames, and again that they correlate with family group. This is because Travellers follow a strict rule[42] of naming the first son and daughter after the father's parents, the second two after the mother's, then after the father's, and mother's, oldest siblings (= the children's great-grandparents' names) with the result that every individual has numerous cousins with the same names as themselves and their own siblings, not to mention their aunts and uncles, nieces and nephews, grandchildren and so on. It is also, coincidentally, why names like Bernard and Julia, that have fallen out of fashion among non-Travellers, are alive and well among particular Traveller families – and not, *nota bene*, common to 'the Traveller community' of which we hear so much. Since intermarriage is tightly confined to the same few surnames, first names circulate too. There is nothing optional about this; breaking the pattern is, as we see in the following extract, a serious move[43]:

> [listing a relative's children]: **Searchas, Treasa, Bidín, Méabh, Neasa, Caitlín.**
> **– You're doing this interview a while now. Do you notice anything strange about that?**

'Types and causes of dispute in an Irish community' in *Éire-Ireland* 3:3 (1968), pp. 27-37; Messenger, *Inis Beag, Island of Ireland* (Illinois, 1983), p.74; C. M Arensberg and S. T. Kimball, *Family and community in Ireland* (Boston, 1968), p. 77, occasionally getting it wrong (Eileen Kane, 'Man and kin in Donegal: a study of kinship functions in a rural Irish and an Irish-American community' in *Ethnology*, 7 (1968) pp. 245-58), with only one –Fox, *The Tory Islanders* (Boston, 1978), p. 66 – pointing out that the concepts are quite distinct, and minutely lexicalised, in Irish, while another (Elliot Leyton, 'Irish friends and "friends"': the nexus of friendship, kinship, and class in Aughnaboy' in Elliott Leyton (ed), *The compact: selected dimensions of friendship* (Newfoundland 1974), pp. 93-104, examines the overlap in detail.

[41] Gmelch, *The Irish Tinkers*, p.31, Helleiner, *Irish Travellers*, p. 180. McCarthy, 'Itinerancy and poverty', p. 43.

[42] One does encounter young Travellers with 'trendy' names, but invariably their birth and baptismal certificates bear the 'correct' one even if it is never used.

[43] Contrast the tone of this dialogue, in which the speaker openly teases me, with the deferential attitude adopted by the 'O'White' woman quoted earlier.

S: Yeah, I notice that there's names there that never showed up before. There's a Méabh and there's a Neasa and Neasa is doubly strange, not only because it never showed up before, but because it's the Irish version of a name[44].
Yes. Anything else?
S: Eh ... Okay, tell me what I'm missing here.
Now, what way should it have started?
S: It should have started ...
The eldest boy is always called after his father's father.
S: Yes! So it should have been Tomás.
That time, she didn't get along with his parents, so she didn't give them the satisfaction of calling the child after them!
S: Fair enough! Yeah! [both laugh] It's all so *human*, isn't it?
This is Treasa, called after *her* mother. Which – these two should have been after *his* mother [sic: parents].
S: These should have been Tomás and Bidín.
Yeah. Which they're not. You see, you have Bidín down there at the end, but she should have been there! So I thought you'd cop that, now!

Pitt-Rivers observes that a child's first name is his individual identity differentiating him from siblings, whereas the surname confers collective social identity; the first and surnames therefore symbolise contrasting forces.[45] But if first names are not individual – if they follow strict guidelines affirming existing kin links, and are habitually coupled with those of other kin – then this dichotomy never emerges: one's identity is 'purely' collective/social. Travellers are securely enmeshed in vast networks of humans living, dead, and as yet unborn, a fact emphasised by the finite and repetitive nature of names through the generations. The tiny pool of recycled first and surnames means that each Martin Ward, each Elizabeth Cash is part of a vast synchronic and diachronic continuum of other Martin Wards and Elizabeth Cashes, within which each also has personality and individuality delineated by nickname/s and by association with relatives (parents, affines, children). Simultaneously, however, this intense interlinkage delineates 'one's own' from the unlinked: each intermarrying cluster effectively comprises a microethnicity which sees itself as distinct, particularly from those with which no intermarriage takes place.[46]

---

[44] It is precisely because Travellers rarely bear Irish first names that I use them as pseudonyms.
[45] Julian Pitt-Rivers, 'The kith and the kin' in Jack Goody, (ed.) *The character of kinship* (Cambridge, 1973), pp. 89-105.
[46] My doctoral research pursued, and confirmed, fundamental differences between intermarrying families in three controversial areas, namely 1. what they call their ethnic language, 2. marriage strategies, and 3. conflict. This paper touches briefly on only one of these, i.e. marriage strategies. I have been unable to find a publisher for the thesis as a whole.

It is only after all the dialogue of getting the family trees that I bring out the tape recorder and ask questions about what I, as a non-Traveller, understand by 'family history'. I undertake this with a basic checklist of topics I would like covered in mind, but in practice the way it works is to introduce an idea and let the person run with it, if they are so inclined. I get the full range of responses, from monosyllabic to self-indulgent rambling to a sort of damburst of reminiscence. But even where the person being interviewed is genuinely open and cooperative, they never – as I pointed out earlier – forget who they are speaking to, or how their words may be used. So I have ended up with masses of data on, for example, work practices in the past, but very little on current economic activities. This reticence stems from well-founded fear that admitting involvement in same might jeopardise social welfare benefits. In fact, I never even ask about work in the present tense, because I know such questions would be seen as a direct threat.

Other topics are off limits for reasons of diplomacy: when I point out that the speaker's family tree includes marriages only with surnames A-D, but not with E-Z, and ask why these families do not intermarry, the response is nearly always some sort of circular reasoning (viz., that the As, Bs, Cs and Ds do not marry the Es and so on because they marry each other). If I push it, and ask how they would feel at the prospect of a child of theirs marrying someone with one of these 'other' surnames, the answer is always along the lines of 'as long as they're happy'. This is an interesting response, as it is what the speaker assumes the researcher wants to hear: it panders to the non-Traveller notion of marriage as the union of two individuals, whereas Traveller marriage, like Traveller identity, is collective; as noted above, each surname typically intermarries with maybe half a dozen other surnames (out of the 200 or so). Now, obviously, these 200 surnames are not all equally numerous, nor are all of them widely dispersed geographically – but many surnames that coexist territorially, do not intermarry. If one were to take what is said in formal interviews at face value, one would also have to accept that the extraordinarily tight colour/surname patterns of Traveller family trees are pure coincidence. Here, by contrast, is what a long-standing friend had to say on such a marriage within her own family:

> **Sometimes my sister married to a [member of an otherwise unlinked family], there's times there when there's a feud[47] going on in my family and**

---

[47] Note that this speaker uses the word 'feud' to describe a verbal quarrel; families who use the term this way do not practise the tit-for-tat interfamily violence classically implied by it, though others – with whom they do not intermarry – certainly do; see Sinéad Ní Shúineár, *Conflict and conflict resolution* (Navan, 2005). Radically diverse ways of handling conflict are among the practical differences between distinct intermarrying surname clusters.

> they'd actually throw that up to my mother: 'Ah, sure, look it, you gave away[48] your lovely daughter to – to that crowd' like. That attitude.
> S: What word would be used? 'You gave away your lovely daughter to –' ? What would people actually say?
> **Sometimes they'd say The Boglanders, or The Galway People. They even call them tramps, sometimes. Any word at all, you know? Like, we think the word 'knacker', when country people call it to us, is very low, very, very low, for someone to call you that. And there's times there when some of the family turn around and say, 'You gave my sister to knackers!' You know that kind of attitude? The attitude that country people would have?**
> S: Mmm.
> **They'd have it towards them strange Travellers.**

In fact there is a world of difference between an interview and good old gossip, where diplomacy is thrown to the winds and the muzzle is off that snide little voice inside each of us that wants to highlight the perceived faults of others. When people stop being 'nice', I get a completely different spin on things. Of course there is a reason families consciously, deliberately avoid intermarriage with most other families: they don't like or trust them, they are just too different to be compatible. Sometimes the accusations are mutual: the As accuse the Bs of marrying their double first cousins, the Bs accuse the As of the same thing, their family trees show that neither does so. Sometimes, though, they tally: the As say that women in the B family run wild, while the Bs say that A women have no personal freedom – different spins on a single theme. Either way, the perceptions are interesting, because they tell us what different families define as objectionable, and (by inference) the model they, and the families they habitually marry in with, espouse. Moreover, they reveal that the bland, circular responses typically given by people I do not know well, are in fact diplomatic silences – so diplomatic, indeed, that without the candid insights of intimate dialogue to compare them with, one would never even recognise them as silences.

Summarising my experiences of collecting Traveller history, it has entailed a fundamental rethink of the very notion of 'history' as a cultural construct. Travellers' accounts of their collective past not only force the researcher to radically reassess preconceived notions of crucial versus irrelevant aspects thereof, but also challenge smug convictions that those of us who record our realities in writing have, by contrast with non-literate cultures, an 'objective' grasp of the people and events that have shaped our present. My initial pursuit

---

[48] This wording misleadingly implies that the young woman in question was 'married off' to a partner of her parents' choosing, whereas in fact they reluctantly consented to her choice of a partner to whom they (and the rest of the extended family) were bitterly opposed, in order to avoid the scandal of an unsanctified 'live together' union.

of 'the' Traveller version of 'the' Traveller past was in itself an ethnocentric will o' the wisp. I came to understand that Traveller reality is subdivided by family group, subject to ongoing discussion, updating and modification with no individual's version definitive, and that its concerns – focusing on the bonds of kinship – are quite different from those (such as group origins) I felt were important and assumed I would find. Reassessing my understanding of Traveller history in turn forced me to critically examine how I, and indeed non-Travellers in general, have a similarly flexible approach to the past despite our illusion that written records give us a firmly grounded grasp of same. With or without such records, humans exercise cultural choice regarding how they define their own collectivities, which aspects of the past are deemed relevant, and how selected aspects are interpreted. And, with or without written records, these choices change over time.

I have also been struck by the radically different quality and depth of information conveyed by friends gossiping over a pint, and when interviewing acquaintances; I have, moreover, become aware of a number of techniques people use to placate an interviewer without alienating or confronting them. I am convinced that these observations apply, not only to all non-Travellers researching Traveller history (and indeed Traveller culture generally) but across the board in intercultural research, historical or otherwise, complicated by a power differential. Rather than condemning vulnerable individuals for 'lying'[49] the researcher should endeavour to understand the deeper truths embodied in what they say – not least when it is blatantly false. The truth within the 'lie' is manyfaceted, ranging from a simple desire to protect one's own and divert negative attention towards one's enemies, to a profoundly different grasp of the issues in question.

Reality itself is inseparable from cultural interpretations thereof. Endeavouring to grasp different versions of ostensibly shared reality is a far more challenging, and rewarding, pursuit than the quest for one's own culturally-determined priorities within other people's cultures.

---

[49] *Viz.*, 'the Irish lie, and lie they do with admirable touches of wit and ingenuity', Nancy Scheper-Hughes, *Saints, scholars and schizophrenics* (2nd ed., California, 1982), p. 11 and Isabel Fonseca, *Bury me standing: the Gypsies and their journey* (New York, 1995), p.15: 'Gypsies lie. They lie a lot – more often and more inventively than other people'.

NAVAN TRAVELLERS WORKSHOPS: TRACING THE TRANSFORMATION FROM ITINERANT SETTLEMENT TO COMMUNITY DEVELOPMENT

MICHAEL MCDONAGH[1]

Navan Travellers Workshops, as we talk about it today, originally would have been known as St. Jude's Committee for Travelling People, though everyone just referred to it as 'The Committee', even when it changed the name to Navan Travellers Committee, then NTW, which is Navan Travellers' Workshops Limited. Only in the last year or two has the term 'NTW' come to replace 'Committee' in everyday talk.

It was set up in 1966, strongly inspired by the Commission on Itinerancy, which issued its Report in 1963. That Report generated a groundswell of interest in what was happening with the Traveller community, but coming very, very much from a charitable approach. A lot of Travellers were living on the roadside at that time in conditions that were totally inhumane, and there would have been a lot of people saying – I don't know what words to use. 'The poor unfortunates', that sort of mentality – 'What can we do to help them?' I'm not saying that's negative, and at that time it was very important. So a number of people in the Meath area came together, and I honestly have to say they were a little bit ahead of their time, because where elsewhere people just got together and said, 'We'll do this, and we'll do this'. Here, before they set the Committee up, they would have done consultation not necessarily with Travellers, but with other groups in the area. They were very strongly linked to St Vincent de Paul, and the Legion

---

[1] This chapter is a transcription of two interviews conducted with Michael McDonagh by Sinéad Ní Shúinéar. The transcript was revised by Michael McDonagh, with input from Anne Hyland, Nell McDonagh, and Paddy Pryle. Acronyms and organisations are explained in the text and footnotes. References to specific people, places and events have been footnoted by the editors.

of Mary, and that type of volunteering, especially around Christmas, in providing practical direct support.²

When the Committee came into being there was quite a small number of Travellers in this area, and the focus was on accommodation. The first scheme that was set up was in the Alexanderaide area, just outside of town, with what was known at the time as 'tigíns' (prefabricated houses), for a number of families; Travellers still live out there, but houses have been built in place of the tigíns.

One of the major changes that affected the Committee was the fairly large influx of families into the area in the mid 1970s. This was about ten years on from the original Report, and it was the beginning of an end, in a sense: prohibition orders and boulders were starting to be put in place, traditional camping sites were beng blocked off right across the country, and Travellers were being slowed down. I say slowed down because they weren't being stopped at that stage. They were still continuing to travel, but were starting to stay longer periods of time in the one place. It wasn't a huge change: Travellers would have always looked for a camp for the winter, and that would have been hopefully for a longer period rather than continuously moving. One of the reasons they came here was because this would have been a prime area for potato picking, which was seasonal, but Navan, being the principal town, became such a base.

I arrived in Navan when I got married, in 1975. At that time, there was an area in the very centre of town which everybody called the car park – it was derelict, just an open piece of ground where the shopping centre is now. That's where we moved on to, and where a lot of Travellers camped. A few years later a Colomban father who used to be a Garda, and who knew people living in the car park from that time, started calling. Eventually four Colomban fathers became regular visitors, and the other three all had years of experience on the missions – China, Peru, the Philippines.³ These men had been affected by the radical change taking place in Catholic thinking at the time. What started off as bible readings, broadened out within two or three weeks to cover issues like the fact that we were living in dire circumstances in the middle of this fast-growing, progressive town. They were getting us to address our own situation, and it was

---

² Established in Ireland in 1921 by Frank Duff, the Legion promoted Catholic values and practices as part of its charitable work. St Vincent de Paul is an international Catholic, lay voluntary organization that helps the poor by visitation in their homes.
³ The Missionary Society of St Columban, an international Catholic missionary congregation. The Society was founded in Ireland in 1916.

these men who were mainly responsible for changing the thinking of the Committee from being – with the height of respect – wealthy people whose weekends were spent giving out blankets and hampers, to Travellers taking control of their own destiny. I remember at one stage the local authority tried to move us, took us to court and we were all fined ten shillings, or was it fifty pence? Either way, people were still counting in shillings at the time. And most of us refused to pay it, because we felt we had done nothing wrong, and because we had this support. Looking back on it now, we owe an awful lot to the thinking of the Colomban Fathers. Colomban Crescent (first group housing scheme in Navan) was called after them.

And one day the Committee pulled a caravan in, with this young man, Cyril Marron his name was. Very strange – whereas the Colomban Fathers introduced themselves, and told us what they were about, Cyril just arrived. I think the reason he was accepted was that he was so scruffy, that people assumed he was a 'go-the-road', a down and out. We were a bit sceptical of him at first, but slowly he got friendly with people – when the fellows went picking spuds, or played cards in the evening, he was with them. He would've been there about a week or two when we discovered he was a Holy Ghost Father, another missionary order, and he had been abroad too, in Sierra Leone.[4] He was doing a sort of placement, a sort of experience, for himself. Living with Travellers, the way they lived, much like these anthropologists that move in and do these sort of 'spy in the wall' situations.

Now, members of the Committee at that time, I have to say, were already very progressive in their thinking, and would have been getting involved with the Travellers in a way that was very good. But when Cyril came, he mixed and lived with Travellers. And on one occasion I'll never forget, some celebration or other was happening, they were going to a pub in the town, and Cyril went with them, naturally. And when they went into the pub, they were all refused, 'We don't serve your type of people here', which was common enough at the time. I remember Cyril saying to me he couldn't understand why they all walked out, and didn't stand their ground. But he stood his ground, and he demanded, then, to know why he wasn't being served. And the answer he got – I'll never forget it! – was, 'I know the likes of you with your fancy talk, and that! You're pretending you're not a Traveller! Out you get!' So, they thought Cyril was a Traveller as well. Maybe it was brushing off on him!

---

[4] The Congregation of the Holy Spirit is a missionary congregation also known as the Spiritans or the Holy Ghost.

Change came through the Colombans first, but Cyril played a major role as well. He wrote up a report of his experiences, and he informed and met with the Committee afterwards. These men brought in the whole concept of community development, of self-determination, of people making choices for themselves, and that reversed the thinking around the approach to working with people from – again, and I stress the point – a charitable concept, to a revolutionary, development-oriented type of thinking. They were instrumental in helping the thinking of the Committee develop in relation to Travellers taking on responsibility for themselves, and allowing that to happen. That was no small step! When you have set up something, and when you've worked really hard for people, and then suddenly it is like – the child is growing up, and it is going! It's very hard, sometimes, to let go of things like that. Special mention is due here for Anne Duddy, who was there from the first meeting that ever took place in the county, and is still involved to this day. She has been a pillar of continuity, and was very receptive to the community development approach when Cyril and them introduced it. She would have been a particularly strong personality on the Committee, and brought other members along with her.

Another person who played a major role at around this time was Aisling O'Leary, who was employed by Meath County Council as a social worker for Travellers. Up until then the whole image of social workers was a woman that was there to look at how you lived, and take your children off you if it didn't suit her. Whereas Aisling came, again, with this whole new Paolo Freire[5] thinking that was brought back from South America and Africa. So she wouldn't have been seen by Travellers as what we knew as a social worker. She approached us, probably for the first time in our lives, as humans who had a role in designing their own destiny.

So Travellers started to get involved, and the first thing that they did was change the name. St Jude was the patron saint of hopeless cases, Travellers being a hopeless case! The name was changed to Navan Travellers Committee. Simple, straightforward, basic. Now, although it was always called *Navan* Travellers Committee, families from Trim, families from different areas in Meath, always involved themselves in it. It's very much a county-wide organisation, so really it should have been called Meath Travellers, but the Navan name stuck.

Around that time they got money to employ someone to work with the Travellers, to help them develop projects and that. Again, this was the Committee being quite progressive, in that they would have been one of the first

---

[5] Paolo Freire, *Pedagogy of the Oppressed* (Harmondsworth, 1972).

in the country to actually employ someone to undertake community development work, although social work training was the nearest you could get in the Republic at the time. Her name was Brigitte Mintern, a lovely woman, who worked a lot with young people, and the adults as well.

When Brigitte left, the post became vacant and was advertised, and Paul Noonan got it. Paul would have been the first qualified, professional youth and community worker that we had ever experienced, and this was a revelation. He also came from Belfast, which would be ahead of the posse around the whole aspect of people being collective in their approach, because of the situation in the North of Ireland. So it was second nature, in a sense, to them.

It was around this time that Maynooth started to run a youth and community workers' professional qualification course, and that Minceir Misli[6], which I think was also well ahead of its time, came into being. It didn't work so well for us, insofar as an all-Traveller organisation frightened people, more so than anything else, at the time; maybe things would work different now. So other people in other parts of the country were starting to think along these lines, but Navan would've been a few steps ahead. And that allowed us, in a sense, to get in to politics at local, national, and even international levels. Our main platform at the time was the National Committee for Travelling People, bringing together all these local committees set up after the Commission, a lot of whose thinking would have been, again, charitable. I'm not saying that in a negative way, I'm saying that that was what they understood. So Navan then started to play very much a leading role.

These new ideas of community development that Cyril had talked so much about, now were being put into practice, because we had a person who was professional, qualified in that area. So the Committee then, taking another step, started to look at linking into FÁS in relation to training. We had no premises at that time, the parish gave us an office, we didn't get a telephone for a while after that, mind you! Still, slowly but surely we started to build it up. So there was all of this development taking place, new things happening. The Committee started then to have to take on different roles.

I would have joined the Committee around 1978-9. It was a voluntary organisation, nothing formal, you just literally turned up on the night, and you became involved. There would have been about four or five Travellers involved

---

[6] Minceir Misli: the first Traveller-only advocacy organisation established in Dublin in the 1980s.

at the time, out of maybe eight or nine hundred in the area, and out of about ten, twelve people active on the Committee. So a good third were Travellers, already, at that stage. Nell McDonagh was one of the first and would have been – what's the opposite of token? By no means passive, she would have been a mover and shaker as far as shaping the organisation goes. She played a very important role, and the fact that she did it cleared the way for other Travellers to come on board do so. Gradually they started to play serious roles on the Committee as well: secretary, and positions that country people[7] had held, and that you looked up to. And *that* was the thinking that was there. It was individuals, the likes of Anne Duddy, James Hayes, Ger Murphy and people like that, who would have been instrumental in trying to get them involved, and supporting them in a very positive way. These were people that I knew well at the time, but there were people before them, the original Committee members we brought together here for the fortieth anniversary.

It was around then that FÁS (Foras Áiseanna Saothair)[8] started getting involved in what was known as teamwork schemes. It wasn't a generally accepted thing in the country at that time: community employment schemes, partnership, social inclusion – that wasn't the talk of the day! When we were at that stage, it was quite radical, you were rocking the boat, in a sense, scraping pennies from everywhere, and looking to charitable organisations to make donations, which was very rare when it came to Travellers. But having said that, we struggled through. For many years the only development work in this area would have been done by Traveller organisations! I mean *nobody* was doing it. There was need for it – major – but at that time, nobody but us would have been doing it at all.

The first Traveller training centre was set up in Ennis in 1977, and others followed. Between support from FÁS and the Department of Education and the Department of the Environment, they provided a twelve-month training period for young people that were missing out. We decided that wasn't what we wanted, exactly, so we set up our own programme, which we called a vocational preparation programme for Travellers, strongly linked to the Youth Employment Agency and Manpower. It was a pilot project providing vocational preparation for twelve months, and then it moved into more mainstream funding through the centres as well. You only were allowed to stay one year in the programme, but we worked it in a way that they actually got two years, and now they get up to three.

---

[7] 'Country people' is the term used by Travellers to identify settled people.
[8] Foras Áiseanna Saothair, government agency for training, work experience and job placement.

We couldn't operate our training centre as a voluntary organisation with people just coming and going, so we became a limited company at that time. The training centre was known as Navan Travellers Workshops, so that's how the name came into being. People say, why 'workshops' when it's actually a community development organisation? It was because of the training centre at the time, we got that name, and never bothered changing it, to be quite honest. It became NTW and that was it.

The Centre, then, took on a number of trainees, I think it was twenty-four at first. The premises was in the VEC (Vocational Education Committee), and that's where it still is, though in much better conditions now than it was then. One of the things that we pushed very strongly from the beginning, because of the involvement and philosophy of the Committee, was the whole development approach. So, you had the usual metalwork, woodwork, literacy, numeracy. But we introduced the whole aspect of personal development, community development, identity, Traveller culture and heritage. You know, these were brand new subjects, in a sense! What was the point, when the main aim of the centre was, get them out, get them into employment? We've been weekly running language classes for young people for twenty years, since the training centre opened. All of that is part and parcel of who you are, and it helps people to create a very positive identity about themselves. And because of that, some of the younger people that went through the centre started to get involved in relation to what was happening with Travellers in the area. So there was very much a ripple effect in that more and more Travellers started to become more and more involved, and it developed and it developed and it developed, from there, as it is today.

NTW probably was, and is, one of the strongest Traveller organisations in the country. And I think that is very much because of the way the Committee was reared, in a sense. How it was moulded, and how it was shaped. Where it had Travellers actively involved, but by no means in any token way. That was a big part of it. Our Board of Directors would have a 50:50 ratio of Travellers to country people, at this stage. And there would have been no problem with Travellers coming onto the committee, or becoming directors, or the chairperson, or whatever the case is. It's not seen as a daunting thing, anymore. And to me that's huge progress.

I became a director of the organisation many, many years ago. My wife, Nell McDonagh, would have been one of the first Traveller directors. When Paul Noonan left the youth and community development position, I applied for it, without any qualifications. I felt that I had huge practical experience, because I worked very closely with Paul on a voluntary basis. Now, to give someone a position like that, at that time you *had* to have qualifications! I had nothing. But I was offered the post, on condition that I would acquire qualifications. So I went into it, and I was a year and a half in it when I applied to Maynooth, and got accepted on the course, which went on for two full calendar years. Not academic years, but winter and summer, every single day, five days a week, full time. So I had to take a leave of absence from my post for the two years, and I went to Maynooth, and I got my qualification, and the Department accepted that. So I ended up as a youth and community worker.

Slowly but surely, as we built up the organisation, we got money for secretaries, youth workers, CE (Community Employment)[9] managers, you know, all that started to happen. So there was need then for someone to manage the project. I could not say at what point that happened. The post, literally, just developed. We then got funding from the ADM (Area Development Management)[10], which was a major thing, a big, giant step for us. That allowed us to buy equipment, it allowed us to employ people, and gave us money for actions.

The parish had always been very generous, in the sense that they had given us an office upstairs in the CYWS (Catholic Young Women's Society) hall. But then they did a survey in the town about what they should be focusing on, and one of the things that came up was that they should be providing more support for Travellers. So eighteen years ago we moved into our current premises, which belongs to the parish, and we work very closely with it. Our pre-school was actually based in a convent before. It's now part of this building, so there's a nominal fee for that room, and that's a contribution of the parish as well. We pay rent at the standard commercial rate for the rest of the building, and we have invested huge amounts in it down the years, for example we converted what had been the priest's stable, into a modern kitchen. It's an ideal premises, beautiful big buildings, smack in the middle of the town, massive public car park in front.

If you come in to our building, you have the lobby, with our logo painted on the wall, and our statement of what we're about. Then there's the reception area, and the first office is for our finance officer, who has a fair amount of work on his hands, because we get funding from a number of statutory and voluntary agencies, government departments, and so on. Our organisation has grown

---

[9] The Community Employment Scheme is managed by FÁS, and is designed to help the long-term unemployed and disadvantaged enter the workforce.
[10] Area Development Management was established by the Irish government and the European Union to manage resources directed at long-term unemployment, and social and economic marginalisation.

unbelievably in forty years, that we have to employ a finance officer, whereas at one time, you could just look at the red lines through everything!

Then you come to the main office, where I work, as the manager, and Anne Hyland works, as secretary. This is the hub; a lot of what happens, happens from here. The third office is where Stephen Walker, our CE supervisor, works from. Next there's the pre-school, a very large room with its own toilets, kitchen, and lovely playground, which I'd say is one of the best-equipped pre-schools in the county. In the country, as a matter of fact. We invest a huge amount in it, because we want it right for the children. The part-time teacher there is Nell McDonagh, and there's three CE participants as well, two in the pre-school itself and one as an assistant on the minibus that collects the children. Upstairs is the office where Sinéad Maguire, who was the main person involved in developing our heritage website, works. She's our information officer. We get phonecalls and letters on a continuous basis, sometimes from students doing papers, or other people, nationally, looking for information about Travellers, and we also respond to the media, locally and nationally. Then there's John McDonagh who coordinates our youthwork programme, and Martin Joe Joyce, who's our community development animator. We use the word animator because he's very good at getting in to areas, and making things happen, developing things out of them, bringing them to life. On the other side of the courtyard is our kitchen, and the workshop where we'll be developing the barrel-top wagon project, and also tin and copper smithing, as part of the heritage aspects of our future plans.

We have other employees in other venues. There's Louise Levins, our Community Health Worker, employed to develop a community rather than an individual response to health issues. She works very closely with our Primary Health Care Programme, involving twelve Traveller women from the county of Meath, operating out of Cannon Row. We work very closely with the visiting teacher service as well, and we run four different after-schools programmes: three in Navan, one in Trim. We're currently in the process of employing an after-schools coordinator. We'll then have two people working off base, but we all get together at staff meetings here on a fortnightly basis.

We also have twenty CE participants who work on a part-time basis, nineteen hours a week, divided up between training and work experience. So you might be on reception, but you would also be *trained* as a receptionist, so that over a period of time you come to a level of competence that you can apply for a position elsewhere, in the big wide world. The idea is, and we take it quite seriously, that people who come through here should not come back. So the *maximum* anyone can do here on CE projects is three years. They're spread out over a range of things, from the heritage project, the youth programme, the men's group, the women's group, and working in the different areas here, the pre-school or whatever the case is.

The training centre, which we set up, and managed for a long number of years, has now been mainstreamed to the Department of Education, which was good for us, it took all that responsibility off our shoulders. We're still on the management committee, but that is now a sub committee of the VEC. There is still massive overlap between us and the training centre, with something like sixty Travellers involved between them. NTW activities are for the *county* of Meath, so anyone in the training centre can participate in what we do here. But it works the other way, too, with NTW using their premises, their skills, their staff, for example we're running a youth diversity programme at the moment, out of the training centre, but we're financing it. We also do a lot of joint activities, for example there's a training day in Drogheda today, around research, people from both NTW and the training centre are attending that.

All of the training centres have things that they do above and beyond their call of duty, for want of a better word. We said we'd do a lot of exchanges. Last year, for example, we had a youth group over in Germany, at the Pope's Mass; we've been to France, Sweden. We brought a group of Travellers to meet Hopi Indians in Nevada, amazing people! We also brought groups on two visits to Irish-American Travellers in Murphy Village, to build up the links there: some of them came back here, and we still get cards and phone calls regularly. I myself have been over three or four times, including one time with a director, Ian Palmer, in the hopes of doing a documentary. Which never materialised, but a lot of good recordings were got from Travellers in America, some of whom are now dead, talking about their lives in America, and their fathers' and grandfathers' lives in Ireland, when they came over, the stories that they brought with them, and the links that still existed. We've some footage as well of some of the customs and traditions of Travellers over there, that would be different from here – slightly! When you look at them right, they're not major differences. Maybe a little more brazen!

The training centre is very linked in to the third age group in Summerhill, particularly the choir. At the other end of the age scale, we set up our first summer project in 1982. At that time Traveller children did not get involved in mainstream provision, they were not accepted and that was the reality of it. We wanted to give them some sort of summer play scheme, and literally, we made it up as we went along, because we hadn't really an awful lot to model ourselves on, and it went down an unbelievable treat. The summer projects were, for the children, very much the main event of their summer, they got involved in crafts, and arts, and organised games, and sport, and swimming, and day trips, and stuff that they would have heard about, but never have taken part in. So here you had parents who would be wary of everything that settled people did, getting involved in something that their children could take part in, and were quite pleased that their children were taking part in.

Our summer project was very culturally sensitive, not that we used those words at the time! Just, the people who were involved in designing it were Travellers, so they knew what was important for their own children, and that's why it worked so well for us. In time, a number of other Traveller organisations around the country – Tullamore, Pavee Point – contacted us asking could they get work experience on our summer projects, so they could set them up in their areas. Which we facilitated. So our project was used as a training ground for others.

We also involved the VSI (Voluntary Services International)[11], volunteers from all over the world who came and worked for the few weeks on these projects. For a lot of the children, it was the first time they sat down and talked to someone from France, or from America, or from Russia, or from China – and that in itself was major. As time went on we didn't necessarily need the international volunteers so much to do the work, but they were very much like icing on the cake, they gave a flavour to it, and the children loved them. Even to this day, some of the adult Travellers still correspond with volunteers that they knew as children. I know one man who is married, has grandchildren! And he actually still gets letters from one of the VSI volunteers. So we've helped build up a lot of friendships.

We then, three years ago, we stopped that, and we celebrated our twenty-first summer project by producing a very good book called *21 Summers* – a collection of photographs, and people's thoughts and memories of the projects over the years – and by bringing the children to Euro Disney, which was a major treat. Next year again we ran a similar project, a pilgrimage to Lourdes. After those two years' break, and coming very strongly from young mothers in particular, who wanted their children to experience what they experienced, we have reverted back to doing our project in the traditional manner, because they felt that that was what they got the most out of. And it's really interesting: we do swimming lessons here for the men's lifestyle change programme, and the

---

[11] Voluntary Services International, the Irish branch of Service Civil International, an international organisation that works for peace through voluntary work and exchanges.

women were asking about it. *All* the women who could swim, learned how during the summer project. Something that you never set out to do, simply happened, and it stays with them. More important again: it broke the ice. They went on to do these things outside of the summer project. To this day, now, lots of the families would have a family membership of the swimming pool, joined the GAA, the soccer, some of them got involved in drama societies, and stuff like that.[12] They started to come out of their shell and become involved in other activities, and other agencies, that they never would have been involved in before. So it had a major effect.

Over the years we have done two plays, made them up from zero. We did one called *Go Move Shift*, about a Travelling family being evicted, at a time when there were the height of difficulties around that area in this town, and it was very successful. Three years ago, as part of our Euro Disney fundraising, we put on a play called *Wedding Belles*, about a young Traveller woman getting married, and her friends who were country people. We had to turn people away from the doors, it was packed to the gills, and it was brilliant, telling a real-life story. And the skill of the people! Just ordinary Travellers, and country people, working together. I would love to start up a drama group, because Travellers have serious skills around drama and music that are not being tapped into. Only recently are you getting a taste of it: Shayne Ward won The X Factor,[13] Chris Doran represented Ireland in the Eurovision.[14] Even in socialising: we often go out to the Rathcairn Gaeltacht[15], it's only up the road from Navan, and they love the Travellers – for their singing qualities! Many's the great sing-song we had out there. So there's huge potential in that area, that we would like to tap into. I've some recordings of Traveller singing made by a man of the name of Tom Munnelly, who has done a lot of collecting. We'd be hoping to do something similar to that, for our heritage website.

The first publication that I can recall would have been *Pride and Prejudice*, which was a teachers' handbook for post-primary civics classes, looking at areas like discrimination – 1986. There was another called *Now and Then*, 1992, and

---

[12] Gaelic Athletic Association, a voluntary, nationwide sports organisation that promotes and organises indigenous games.
[13] A 20-year old from Manchester, Ward won a United Kingdom television talent contest in December 2005.
[14] On 15 May 2005, Chris Doran represented Ireland at the Eurovision Song Contest.
[15] Rathcairn Gaeltacht is an Irish-speaking area in County Meath that was established by the government in 1935, when families from Connemara, County Galway were re-settled in Meath.

another, *Travellers, Their Life and Times,* 1996, a booklet to go with a tape of songs and stories and talking. They all were very important, but the publication of *Conflict and Conflict Resolution* in 2005 was a milestone. All the other publications that we'd done – for example, *21 Summers*, a collection of photographs and stories, all positive, all happy, the craic, *Life and Times* was heritage – they were distant, and yet part of you. *Conflict and Conflict Resolution* was *close*. It wasn't looking back, it was looking *inside*, at a part of Travellers' lives that Travellers were very cagey about looking at. Cagey is putting it quite mildly – some of them were petrified! People literally put their heads on the chopping block. That's the reality of it, and I have great admiration for them, because they needed to do something to change, for them and their children, and they did it. It was a major breakthrough, and I am so proud of them, to be quite honest with you. That publication now is being used in other areas, other organisations are contacting us on the need to do workshops on how to look at conflict, and the more that do that the better for Travellers, because we will start to deal with conflict in ways that don't result in us having to engage in a violent act. All along there's been mediation services on conflict between Travellers and settled people, which is horrible, and difficult, but compared to conflict between Travellers it is a cinch to address. The other one is so close to the bone, and whether you like it or not, you are part of it. So, to me that was a major piece of work.

Over the years we've had a number of different hands-on projects, and one of the major ones, that I would like to see revived, was the caravan repair and fire safety programme. At that time a lot of Travellers were buying mobile homes and caravans that were designed for a middle-class family to holiday in for two or three weeks in the warm weather, not for rearing a family in wintertime. Travellers started fitting in solid fuel stoves and stuff like that, and a lot of the time asbestos was being used, as well, which was quite dangerous in itself. They weren't being done properly, and they were becoming tinderboxes, because when you've a fire inside something that was never meant to have a fire, it dries it up completely, so the least little thing – it just literally, exploded, and very rarely did you have survivors. Every area of the country was affected by this. We had two, three people burnt to death in caravans in this area. So we set up this project, and the outcome of it was that a lot of the local authorities we dealt with introduced proper fire-fighting equipment, firewalls and so on, to their halting sites. People can also now rent, or buy, caravans from the local authorities the same way they can buy or rent houses, so they looked safer ways of doing it. We trained people in to work with the local authority on inspections: making sure caravans were fitted properly, and also to repair and refit, which was never done before. The project didn't continue, largely because the

European funding didn't continue, and as far as I know, inspection of caravans from the fire safety point of view is not being done anymore. It is one project that I always have at the back of my mind that I would love to see brought back, because clearly what happened in Clondalkin there a short time ago shows us that those concerns have not gone away.[16]

We've a lot of different projects! We have been innovative in a lot of ways, for example the recent healthy eating programme, the cooking programme for the women here. Our latest one is a driving course for women, country women and Traveller women taking it together, and that's going extremely well. It has a twofold effect: everyone's getting a licence, but also, it's building up a relationship. The day the women went, all eighteen of them, for the theory test, that was the first time for quite a number of them that they ever passed any sort of a state exam. So it's not just a driving programme, it is confidence and self-esteem that we're working with as well. We will be trying to target a number of them, when the driving course is over, to get involved in the board of management here. It's give and take.

Even for the men, which – it is very difficult to get men involved! We've a men's lifestyle change programme, which is working well, and I'm really pleased with that. It involves swimming, and cooking – they're also involved in healthy eating – and every second week now they have someone in from the Health Board giving them talks on different aspects of health: blood pressure, cancers, cholesterol, all of that range of stuff. And it's starting to have an effect on them, and I think that's brilliant!

The National Travellers' Art Competition was begun about three or four years ago, by the NATC (National Association of Travellers' Training Centres), which is the national organisation. Navan Travellers Training Centre, as a local organisation, said, 'Okay, we will help to make this happen.' Because you need a base, and you need continuity, to make things like this happen. So we are heavily involved in that, and it has been a huge success. It has attracted paintings, photographs, sculpture, from Travellers all over – north and south, Belfast, Derry.

That's some of what's happening at the moment, but we also have future plans. We are in the very lucky position of getting a gift of some land, and the plan is to use it for a national Traveller heritage park that would give visitors a feel for what it was like to live as a Traveller, as well as an organic farm, a restaurant,

---

[16] See *Irish Times*, 28 Nov. 2005.

and stabling for horses.[17] We're currently building our first barrel-top wagon here, but when we get the land we'll be working from there, making barrel-tops, maintaining them, keeping horses, and renting them out to tourists. Meath has a huge potential for tourism that's not being tapped into. This sort of thing has been done – not by Travellers! – in other areas that are quite hilly, and yet here you have a very flat county, ideal for this type of thing, and nothing like this. So we'll be linking into the Meath tourism board. We'd want to set up sites as well, where they can pull these in. We're also looking at the possibility of a community radio station. It would be a brilliant opportunity to get people involved, as well as getting the message out without having to compromise the message too much to do so.

We recently had our fortieth anniversary celebration, and that was a major event. We had a number of goals for it, the first being that we wanted to give recognition to the people that originally started the whole thing, by bringing them together, and thanking them, and giving them an opportunity to meet people who came on board ten, twenty, thirty years after them, so they could see who they'd passed the torch on to. These are people who are now in their seventies and eighties. It must have been a very positive feeling for them to see that what, at the time, they might have felt was a small input, was major, and the fruits of that are now being borne. We gave a presentation of a beautiful miniature glass cart on a wooden base, to the original Committee members. Travellers made those carts for them, but working in glass wouldn't be something that Travellers traditionally did, so it was also symbolic of introducing new skills.

There was also the launch of our website, the first ever national Travellers' heritage website (http://www.travellerheritage.ie). There are lots of old photographs on it, set up in a way that people can click into their family name, as well as stories, folklore, history, songs, cures, recipes. We are already getting huge amounts of letters and phonecalls from Travellers saying, 'How can I get this photograph? or, 'Put this photograph up!' This is brilliant, it's exactly what we wanted. So, it is having the desired effect.

There was also the opening of the playground for our pre-school, and food for three hundred prepared by Traveller women on our healthy eating programme. We didn't get politicians in for the occasion, although I think we easily could have, but we purposely didn't because we wanted to keep it local. You had the people who were involved on the Committee, you had the Travellers, and then

---

[17] Developments reported on in *Irish Times*, 30 Mar. 2006.

you had Joe Public, and Josephine Public. We had a beautiful barrel-top wagon out the front, in the main road, and that created a lot of discussion, people coming along to have their photograph taken in front of what at one time would have had them saying, 'Oh, my God, here's the tinkers'. I thought it was a lovely change! They just came in to see what was going on, and they were every bit as important to be there as anybody else, because at the end of the day, that's who's out there, and that's who we're trying to get across to, and we did get across to them.

So the open day was important for a lot of reasons other than simply saying thank you. The publicity was very positive, and the ongoing impact of that publicity has been very positive as well. We're actually quite skilled, at this stage, of sensing where we're wanted and where we're not wanted, and you can feel the different atmosphere. I remember doing church gate collections in the past, and you would spend most of your time defending your existence, and put up with abuse, and then they'd walk away without putting a penny in the box. We did the church gate collection here a couple of weeks ago, well after the open day, and the amount of people who said, 'Well done! You're doing good work! and donating a substantial amount of money. To me, that says a lot about where people are coming from: putting their hands in their pockets, and supporting us. So a lot of that came out of it, and also the 'feel-good' factor, of feeling very positive about your identity. That was important for everybody. So for me it was a win/win day.

We're not great at writing things up. See, you just *do* things, do them because they have to be done, and you never *count* them. It's hard to remember them all, and tag them with the dates. We would be involved in a lot of other stuff in this area, that's nothing to do with Travellers, necessarily. Like the County Development Board[18], we have representation on that, the County Childcare Committee, RAPID[19] – revitalisation of local authority estates – where a lot of Travellers live, and that's why we're involved in it. There is recognition that Travellers in this area, have, over the years, learnt a huge amount of skills in community development, and we're sharing them with the settled people. Travellers are now chairpersons of some of the tenants' associations, which were our arch enemy at one time! They were always campaigning against Travellers, and now Travellers are chairpersons of these organisations. That's a

---

[18] In 2000, thirty-four County Development Boards were established to synthesise the work of local development bodies, the community and voluntary sector, state agencies and local elected members.
[19] Revitalising Areas by Planning Investment Development, a government programme focusing on disadvantaged communities

complete change around. And I had to laugh to myself going past one of the pubs in this town the other day, a Traveller working as the doorman, saying who gets in! And there are loads of Travellers who are taxi drivers in this town. It's that type of change around that's taking place. But – the important thing – all of this is being done without having to deny who you are. Sadly, in some areas, that haven't had the support and backup of an organisation such as ourselves, they had to lose it, to make it – if you want to call it 'making it'. Here, you don't have to lose your identity.

NTW Timeline

1966 St Jude's Itinerant Settlement Committee established
First provision of accommodation for Travellers: 4 'tigíns' (prefab chalets) at Alexanderaide

1967-1973 Committee engaged in general support and charitable work

1974 First Traveller family in council house in Meath

1975 Traveller families move into carpark, Navan town centre
First Traveller family in Navan local authority housing estate
Preschool playgroup (3-5 year olds) set up

1976 Meath gets its first social worker for Travellers

1977 Committee helps Travellers fight trespass prosecutions
Community development approach replaces social work
Adult education classes include literacy and cookery

1981 Youth and community worker hired

1982 Meath County Council takes residents' association to High Court for blocking its work on group housing for 12 families in St Colomban's Crescent; families move in in December.
First summer project

1983 'NTW' name adopted

1986 Committee employs researcher to explore enterprise ideas for the Travelling community

	Publication, *Pride and Prejudice. The Case of the Travellers*, a teachers' handbook for postprimary civics
1987	Overview of work to date lists workshop, preschool, 'Navan Car Care' 20 on employment programme, 17 on Teamwork employment schemes, Traveller facilitated to attend fulltime university diploma course
1989	Publication, *Profile and Survey of Traveller Needs in Navan*
1990	St Patrick's Park Halting Site (14 families) Reask Court group housing (4 families) NTW issue statement deploring orchestrated movement opposing Traveller accommodation
1992	Publication, *Now and Then*
1993	NTW hosts meeting of European Gypsy/Traveller Education Group, with representatives from 9 European Union Member States
1994	First exchange visit to Irish-American Travellers in Murphy Village, USA Beaufort College (Navan) boycott: all students withdrawn in protest at alleged harassment from nearby Traveller camp; Travellers evicted. Original play, *Go Move Shift*, staged
1995	Residents action group mounts round-the-clock vigil to prevent work on site for 14 families at Windtown; it goes ahead
1996	Publication: *Travellers, Their Life and Times* (booklet accompanying cassette tape of songs and stories)
1997	Families move in to Windtown site
1998	Newsletter, *Luba on the Grage*, with jobs columns and coverage of after-schools, literacy course, summer project
1999	Meath gets its first visiting teacher for Travellers Training

	centre exchange visits with Sweden Senior women's group visits Black inner city high school in Philadelphia, USA
2000	Typical overlap project: 'Tiffney Glass Works' – NTW-based CE workers use training centre facilities
2003	Publications, *Stand Up Sit Down* (Traveller and non-Traveller children collaborate on a book about friendship and conflict) and *21 Summers* celebrating summer projects Original play, *Wedding Belles*, part of fundraising for Euro Disney trip which takes place this year
2004	Pilgrimage to Lourdes
2005	Publication, *Conflict and Conflict Resolution*
2006	Delegation to World Youth Day, Cologne, Germany

Chapter Seven

Shelta: Historical and Sociolinguistic Aspects

Alice Binchy

This paper will examine historical references to Shelta, assess its relationship to Cant and offer some hypotheses as to how it should be regarded from a sociolinguistic perspective.

Cant and Shelta

The term 'Cant' refers to at least three separate entities: first, cant as a synonym for argot or jargon; second, a specific code called English Cant, or the Canting language; and, third, the language which academics call Shelta and many Irish Travellers call Cant. Shelta has previously been treated as belonging to the class of cant in the first sense, partly because of its treatment at the hands of those who first wrote about it but also because of the fact that Travellers were traditionally viewed as being deviant members of mainstream society rather than as a distinct group.

To separate out these strands, it is necessary to go back to the early sixteenth century, when the first group of Gypsies arrived in England, representing themselves as religious refugees from the Middle East (the name 'Gypsy' being a corruption of Egyptian) and speaking their own language, Romani. England at that time supported a sizable population of wandering vagabonds, outcasts and criminal gangs. Over time, as the nomadic Gypsies established themselves and lived alongside the native nomads, the majority, settled, population came to class them all as one group. This early mixing of the two distinct groups may have given rise to the notion that the Romani language was itself specifically contrived to facilitate criminality, and until the early eighteenth century it was thought to be a made-up jargon. Research by a German scholar, Heinrich Grellman, published in English by Hoyland in 1816 showed that the ultimate origin of the group was India rather than Egypt and that their language, Romani, had its roots in a number of Indian languages, including Sanskrit.[1] The difference between the Gypsies and other groups who were on the road at the same time became clear, at least to linguists if not to the general public

A contemporary commentator, Harison (1577) suggests that the native vagrants, rather than mixing and intermarrying with the Gypsies, set up in opposition to them, adopting some of their practices, including that of speaking a distinct language:

> Moreover, in counterfeiting the Egiptian roges they have devised a language among themselves, which they name canting, but others pedlar's French, a speech compact thirtie years since of English and a great number of od words of their oown devising, without all order and reason: and yet such is it that none but themselves are able to understand. The first devisor thereof was hanged by the necke, a just reward for his deserts, and a common end to that profession.[2]

The first written reference to what may be called English Cant was in 1566, when the magistrate Harman published a work based on his experiences on the bench. He described the various categories of rogue, gave examples of Cant and commented on its emergence:

> As far as I can learn or understand by the examination of a number of them, their language – which they term peddelars French or Canting – began but within these xxx yeeres or lyttle more.[3]

Harman's work was followed by the first formal glossary of Cant, *A New Dictionary of the Canting Crew*, published anonymously in 1698. The next work of importance was Captain Francis Grose's *Classical Dictionary of the Vulgar Tongue* in 1785, which is considered by Mencken to be the basic text for students of cant and slang.[4] John Camden Hotten's *Slang Dictionary* (1864) was the last to include Shelta words without identifying them as such. Hotten attributes words like *tober* 'road' and *granny* 'ring' to what he calls Old Cant; Shelta's existence had not then been publicised. Later slang dictionaries, for example Partridge correctly identify these and other items as Shelta.[5]

---

[1] J. Hoyland, *Survey of British Gypsies* (London,1816)
[2] C.J. Ribton-Turner, *A history of vagrants and vagrancy and beggars and begging* (London,1887) p. 466
[3] T. Harman, *A caveat for common cursetors, vulgarly called vagabones* (Reprinted in Salgado, G. *Cony Catchers and Bawdy Baskets,* 1972)
[4] H. Mencken, *The American Language* (London 1963), p. 71.
[5] E. Partridge, *Dictionary of Historical Slang* (Harmondsworth,1972)

Shelta first came to academic attention in the 1880s when Charles Leland wrote of coming across an Irish Traveller in England who mentioned to him another language that was far older than Romani and was habitually spoken by Irish Tinkers, as they were then called.[6] This informant called the language Sheldhru (which Leland rendered Shelta) and in his excitement Leland described it as a fifth Celtic language, maybe even the lost language of the Picts. Before long, amateur folklorists were filling the pages of the *Journal of the Gypsy Lore Society* with sightings of Irish Travellers and specimens of their language. Most of these specimens were collected outside Ireland, although it was generally accepted that the language was the property of Irish Travellers and was not related to Romani. The language included elements from Irish (old as well as modern) and English, and some which scholars were not able to identify.[7] It was termed the 'secret language' of tinkers or Travellers, reflecting the belief that its speakers were an occupational sub-group of the mainstream population, who needed a special vocabulary to communicate exclusively with their own group.

The issue now is the relationship between Cant and Shelta. The people who spoke English Cant were considered a sub-division of the majority population, and the Cant language was considered a sub-division of the majority language. But who exactly were these people? Borrow described them as called:

> ... in the old cant language Abraham men, and in the modern Pikers. These people have been frequently confounded with the Gypsies, and like them they have a kind of secret language. But the Gypsies are a people of oriental origin, whilst the Abrahamites are the scurf of the body corporate. The language of the Gypsies is a real language ... whereas the speech of the Abrahamites is a horrid jargon, composed for the most part of low English words used in an allegorical sense [8]

The questions to be answered now are: what proportion of the non-Gypsy wanderers in Britain over the centuries was Irish, whether they were Travellers, and what proportion of English Cant was in fact Shelta. The term Abraham or Abram men denoted wanderers who pretended to be mad, who were driven onto the road by the dissolution of the monasteries.[9] Borrow says the term comes from 'old cant' which is also the source, as noted earlier, of some terms which are clearly Shelta. Ribton-Turner (1887) gives the origin of Abram man as the Irish *bramanach* 'a noisy fellow'. A young thief in Salford jail, who gave

---

[6] C. G. Leland, *The Gypsies* (Boston, 1882).

[7] J. Sampson, 'Tinkers and their talk' in *JGLS,* 2, (1891), pp 204-21. K. Meyer, 'On the Irish origin and the age of Shelta', in *JGLS*, 2, (1891), pp 257-66.

[8] G. Borrow, *Lavengro* (London, 1851).

[9] J. C. Hotten, *The Slang Dictionary* (London, 1864). Grose, *Classical Dictionary.*

Ribton-Turner valuable assistance on the different types of Cant gave as his opinion that:

> ...three parts of those who are travelling now throughout the kingdom, have Irish blood in them, either from father or mother or grandmother.[10]

It becomes clear that what was treated as one cohesive group, speaking one language, could in fact be broken down into three components. Two of them were ethnic, the Gypsies and the Irish (there is not yet enough evidence that they were Travellers) and the third was social, namely the English vagabond class. It is suggested that their languages could likewise be distinguished, as ethnic or social, but more evidence is needed.

Legislation in Britain to deal with influxes of Irish beggars goes back many centuries: *gwestwr*, vagabonds who were considered a public nuisance before 1330, were of Irish and Welsh origin and spoke 'English cant'.[11] Barrere and Leland mention that Irish wanderers were ridiculed as a common type in plays and broadsides in the eighteenth century; and Williams cites a law dated 1654 which ordered the arrest of all wanderers of both sexes and 'other Irish' who had no settled means of support.[12]

Kenrick considering the question of the identity of Irish Travellers, claims that while the Irish against whom British laws on vagrancy were enforced in the Middle Ages were not necessarily all Travellers, there is evidence that Travellers were included.[13] Certainly there is plenty of evidence of Irish influence in records of English Cant. Hotten notes that many English Cant words come from Scottish Gaelic and Irish, but he is not sure if this came about through the settled Irish, who formed part of the lowest class in England, or through 'Irish wanderers' (i.e. Travellers) who formed part of the criminal class.[14] Barrere and Leland take the argument a stage further when they suggest that the majority of words in 'old canting' are Celtic in origin, and that, in modern Cant, most of the Celtic terms do not come directly from Irish, Scottish Gaelic or Welsh, but via Shelta, 'which is spoken by a very large proportion of all provincial tinkers ... as well as by many other vagabonds, especially by all

---

[10] Ribton-Turner, *A history of vagrants*, p. 245
[11] Ibid., p. 467
[12] A. Barrere and C.G. Leland, *A dictionary of slang, jargon and cant* (London, 1897) p.xi. J.J. Williams, *Whence the 'Black Irish' in America?* (New York, 1932), p.12
[13] D. Kenrick, 'How old are the Irish Travellers? Occasional papers of the Romani Institute, 2, (1979)
[14] J.C. Hotten, *The slang dictionary* (London, 1864)

the Irish who are on the roads'.[15] It is interesting to note that most of the early documented examples of Shelta, between 1880 and the 1930s, were collected in Britain. Sampson and MacRitchie confirm that Shelta was widely spoken in England as well as Ireland.[16]

Writing about Scottish Tinklers, as they were called, Sampson claims that their Cant is composed of 'debased Gypsy' and Elizabethan Cant, as used by dramatists like Fletcher, Greene and Dekker.[17] Simson quotes a Scottish traditional belief that, before the death of James II in 1460, gangs of 'Saracens or Gypsies' from Ireland roamed through Galloway in Scotland; and he comments that all the Scottish Gypsies claim that their ancestors came to Scotland from Ireland.[18] Since there is no evidence of Gypsy migration to Ireland at the time referred to (which was before the earliest records of Gypsies anywhere in the British Isles), and since it has been shown that Irish Travellers are not related genetically to Gypsies it may be postulated that these 'Saracens or Gypsies' were the ancestors of today's Irish Travellers.[19] If they were, then it is possible that they spoke Shelta. It seems a reasonable inference, furthermore, that Shelta had some input into the Elizabethan Cant element which Sampson identifies in the language of Scottish Tinklers.

In illustration of this point, compare the following words from Harman's *Caveat for Common Cursetors* with words in daily use by Travellers in Ireland today:

Harman's Cant		Cant/Shelta	
pek	'meate'	**pek**	'food'
lybbege	'bed'	**lee**	'bed'
yaram	'milke'	**yorum**	'milk'
togemans	'a cote, a cloak'	**tugs**	'clothes'
ken	'a house'	**keina**	'a house'
booget	'a traveling tinker's basket'	**budget**	'a tinsmith's box of tools'
chete	'a thing'	**chat**	'a thing'[20]

---

[15] Barrere and Leland, *A dictionary of slang*, p.xi.
[16] J. Sampson 'A hundred Shelta sayings in the Ulster dialect', in *JGLS,* 1, pp 272-77. D. MacRitchie, 'Irish tinkers and their talk', in *JGLS*, 2, pp. 350-57
[17] J. Sampson, 'Shelta or Sheldhru', in Chambers' Encyclopedia, 9, (1893), p. 389
[18] W. Simson, *A history of the Gypsies* (London, 1865), p.55
[19] M.H. Crawford, 'Genetic affinities and origin of Irish Tinkers' in *Biosocial interrelations in population adaptation* (ed.) Watts, Johnson & Lasker, (The Hague, 1976)
[20] T. Harman, *A caveat for common cursetors, vulgarly called vagabones.*

Ribton-Turner points out that while English Cant includes Irish, Welsh and Scottish words, as well as Latin and French, it also includes English motivated expressions such as *grunting chete* (literally grunting thing) 'a pig'; *crashing chetes* (literally crashing things) 'teeth'; *waddler* 'a duck'. This is similar to the jargon stage of pidgin language development, where descriptions are used before names for things, names only developing out of the descriptions though regular usage.[21] These terms bear the marks of a deliberately constructed language.

The words quoted from Harman, which are still in use today, cannot be explained in the same way. If those who spoke English Cant were in contact with Irish Travellers, then Shelta seems to offer a reasonable source of explanation. Sampson's comment on the age of Shelta supports this interpretation:

> The remote origin of this jargon is attested, not only by the universal tradition of the people, but by the number of Shelta words which have passed into English cant (i.e. old slang), some as early as the middle of the sixteenth century [22]

Before it was known that Irish Travellers and Tinkers had a language of their own, Shelta may have been subsumed into references to English Cant. One may speculate that either vagrants, tramps or Tinkers in Britain spoke both Cant and Shelta, or the distinction between the two languages was not clearly drawn. There is widespread support for the view that the Cant language was formed by outcast groups at the time of the Gypsies' first appearance in Britain, in response to their use of Romani.

It is arguable that Irish Travellers contributed part of their language to English Cant, while retaining parts of it as their own preserve. We know that they were in Britain; we know that they had a language of their own; and elements of that language appear in English Cant, in modern times as well as in Harman's day.[23] I suggest that Irish Travellers shared some parts of their language with the other non-Gypsy wanderers with whom they were associated by the majority population, and with whom they shared a way of life but that they kept the largest part of their language from these associates, with the result that the language was not heard of at all until the 1880s.

---

[21] S. Romaine, *Pidgin and creole linguistics* (London,1988), p.36.
[22] J. Sampson 'Shelta or Sheldhru', in Chambers' Encyclopedia, 9, p. 204.
[23] K. Chesney, *The Victorian underworld* (Harmondsworth, 1972)

Shelta and English

A Traveller man in his thirties, interviewed in the 1990s, said:

> I don't think there's ere a Traveller, on the road or off the road, no matter where they're reared, even if they're reared in houses, they still continues to use the language. Parents still teach them the language, they still use it when they're mixing with their own ... Travellers travelling around use it more because they're mixing with more Travellers. There's lots of cases where years ago, people were housed and children grew up with settled children, and even talked like settled children, sounded like them, but still they'd know Cant as well, the parents would make sure they learned the Cant. There'd be occasions where they'd meet relations that still travelled, and they'd be able to make themselves understood in the Cant. That's one thing that's different between Travellers and settled people, Travellers always know Cant. If they didn't, you'd regard them as settled. No matter how long they're in a house ... they still use it.[24]

Travellers refer to Cant as a language. In their view they have a language of their own which they distinguish from English. They do not consider it to be a variety of English. Cant, or Shelta as I call it (to indicate that I am writing about it from outside the Traveller community) shares its grammar and syntax with English. Most of the early commentators on Shelta called it a jargon or slang, partly because they believed that Travellers were an occupational group, but also because they saw Shelta as bearing the same relationship to English as slang. At a superficial level this appears to be so, because Shelta replaces only the lexical items in an utterance, as slang does.

So are Travellers wrong to believe that they have a language? The definition of what is and what is not a language has as much to do with social, historical and political factors as it does with linguistic ones. Some languages which share grammar and syntax are nevertheless considered to be separate entities: for example, Hindi and Urdu are accepted as distinct languages even though they share the same grammatical structure, because they are spoken by groups which are distinct socially and historically. Although they are clearly distinct socially, Travellers have not been recognised as distinct legally, historically or culturally, so it is not surprising that their language would not be considered as being distinct from the Hiberno-English spoken by the majority population.[25]

---

[24] A. Binchy, 'The status and functions of Shelta' (D. Phil, thesis, University of Oxford, 1993)
[25] A. Binchy 'Traveller culture and ethnicity: implications for social policy'. Paper presented at *Travellers, Society and the Law* conference, Trinity College Dublin, July 1997

Empirical research on Shelta which I carried out between 1983 and 1993 has persuaded me that Shelta is a distinct language, as opposed to a variety of Hiberno-English. Reasons for this include the fact that it is transmitted from parent to child, as a joint first language, and that it functions as an ethnic marker for Travellers.[26]

The question of why Shelta does not have an independent grammatical structure is an interesting one. It is possible that at some period in the past Shelta had a distinct grammatical and syntactic structure; there is some academic support for this.[27] If that is so, then, in my view, there are two possible reasons why it disappeared, both related directly to the way Travellers live.

All the historical evidence indicates that Travellers over the centuries were service providers for the majority population. This means that they would have had to speak at least the rudiments of the languages spoken by their customers or clients. It may be that at some point in history Travellers were trilingual, speaking what could be called old Shelta (with a grammatical structure of its own), as well as Irish and English. Each of the three would have had its own role and domains of usage in Traveller life. In similar situations around the world, this has led to the grammars of several distinct languages converging, in the sense that grammatical differences between them are evened out and disappear. As the sociolinguist Suzanne Romaine has said:

> When a situation exists where all the speakers are constantly using all the languages available to them, they lessen the psychological load of having separate systems by allowing them to merge.[28]

It is possible that this is what happened with Shelta. The most compelling evidence in support of this is that exactly the same pattern, of replacing only the lexical items in a sentence or utterance, exists in modern Anglo-Romani, as spoken by the British Romani or Gypsy population. Compare

Anglo-Romani   The **rackli chor**ed the **luvva** [29]
Cant (Dublin 1983)   The **lakin beeg**ed the **greid** [30]
                        The girl   stole   the money

---

[26] Binchy, 'The status and functions of Shelta',
[27] R.A.S. Macalister, *The secret languages of Ireland* (Cambridge, 1937), p.138
[28] S. Romaine, *Bilingualism* (Oxford, 1989), p.163
[29] D. Kenrick 'Romani English' in *Romani Sociolinguistics* ed. Ian Hancock, (The Hague, 1979)
[30] A. Binchy, 'Shelta: an historical and contemporary analysis' (M.A. thesis, National Institute for Higher Education, Dublin, 1985)

British Gypsies live in very similar social circumstances to Irish Travellers, and their relations with their settled neighbours are broadly similar. In their case, however, there is documentary evidence that their language once had a distinct grammatical structure, and its decline can be traced through examples of the language collected over the past three hundred years.[31] That is one possible explanation, based on what we know about Travellers' historical relations with the majority population. The other possibility is more speculative and has at its centre the Traveller tradition of nomadism. This explanation draws on the relatively new area of pidgin and creole linguistics.[32] It seems fairly obvious that for language to develop, there has to be some unity of purpose. In the case of pidgin languages, which develop where there has been no common language, there is agreement about the need to communicate, even in a very basic way. Pidgin languages are culture-neutral since they aim to cross cultural barriers. They eliminate features which would convey only social information relevant to members of the same speech community. Creoles, on the other hand, develop from a combination of cultural and environmental factors. Cultural environment is not only the trigger, but also a constituent in the growth of grammar.[33]

When a pidgin develops, all the strategies adopted by its speakers are geared towards ease of communication across cultural and linguistic barriers. Grammar is not essential for basic communication, as any monoglot English speaker who has travelled abroad knows. When a pidgin language develops into a creole, that is, when it becomes the first language of children born to pidgin-speaking parents, and when it becomes the language of a closed communication network, grammatical devices evolve which have the effect of categorising members into social groups. Grammar becomes a means of signaling membership of the group and relative status within it.

For grammar to develop, there has to be community.[34] LePage and Tabouret-Keller suggest that grammar does not develop unless or until creole speakers commit an 'act of identity' by which they identify their language as the

---

[31] Hoyland's work is an example of this; a more recent debate on the history of the Romani language and its relationship with English, between Donald Kenrick and Ian Hancock, is contained in *Romani Sociolinguistics* (The Hague, 1979)

[32] Pidgin languages are speech forms which do not have native speakers, being used for communication between groups who have no common language. Creole languages, in contrast, have native speakers, and come about when children are born into pidgin-speaking communities. Creole languages have the developmental characteristics of natural languages, while pidgin languages, being simplified in form and function do not.

[33] P. Muhlhausler, *Pidgin and creole linguistics* (Oxford, 1986)

[34] Ibid.

language of a community.[35] Close daily interaction leads a community's language to become focussed, meaning that individual, once-off usages are replaced by rule-based grammar. The more interaction there is within a community, the more prescriptive their grammatical, as well as social, rules will be. The existence of a community is necessary for the development of grammatical rules.

The term community, as used in the field of sociolinguistics, usually has as a primary feature of 'shared location'. But can there be a sense of community without shared location, and, if so, what are the consequences for language? It may be that the definition of community has been weighted in favour of sedentary groups. While other racial, ethnic or occupational groups can, if they wish, live in a community together, this option, both by definition and by the way the norms of sedentary society impact on them, is not open to those who call themselves Travellers. It is clear, however, that, although they live and travel in small family groups, all Travellers owe allegiance to the greater community of Travellers. Travellers use Shelta as a social index to locate unknown or unrelated Travellers. The nature of their society (extended family groups) and their preference in terms of accommodation (mobile rather than fixed) interact to make living in a community impossible.

Nomadism is one of the ways by which small Traveller groups retain faith with the larger Traveller community. It is the reason why some Travellers would willingly live all their lives in a caravan in one spot, but would not live in a house in the same spot. Travelling itself is not as important as remaining disposed to travel. The social setting of Shelta is small family groups, nomadic islands in a sedentary sea, signaling to each other across that sea and united by the collection of habits and dispositions that is Traveller culture.

My hypothesis is that nomadism has caused Shelta to develop as it has: that the small scale of Travellers' daily interactions with their own group was not enough to allow Shelta grammar to be maintained. In the present system, lexicon is the ethnic marker and grammar represents the parts of life shared with settled society. As Ross has pointed out, 'it is precisely the words of a language which are perceived by its speakers as its substance and therefore as the emblem of identity'.[36]

---

[35] R. LePage & A. Tabouret-Keller, *Acts of identity* (Cambridge, 1985).
[36] M.D. Ross, 'A contact-induced morphosyntactic change in the Bel language of Papua New Guinea' in *Pacific Linguistics,* C-100, Canberra, Australian National University, pp. 583-601.

The Travellers I interviewed in the course of my research had an average Shelta vocabulary of about 200 words. This is not a large vocabulary, but a language spoken by a close-knit group, where blood relationships are underpinned by marriage alliances between certain families, does not need to be as complex as one spoken by a more disparate group. Because it is a largely unwritten, face-to-face language, the immediate context, tone, gestures and facial expression can carry supplementary information. Because of shared background knowledge, there is much that does not need to be said in Shelta.

Contributors

Dr Ciara Breathnach is a lecturer at the Department of History, University of Limerick. She has recently published *The Congested Districts Board of Ireland, 1891-1923: poverty and development in the West of Ireland* (Dublin, 2005). She is currently editing a forthcoming volume on visual history *Framing the West* for Irish Academic Press.

Dr Aoife Bhreatnach is a graduate of University College Cork and De Montfort University. She has held the Irish Government Senior Scholarship at Hertford College, Oxford and an Irish Research Council for the Humanities and Social Sciences Post-Doctoral Fellowship at NUI Maynooth. Her monograph *Becoming Conspicuous: Irish Travellers, Society and the State, 1922-70* (2006) is published by UCD Press.

Julie Brazil, holds an MA in Art and Architecture and is a PhD student at the Department of History, University of Limerick. Her current study focuses on the representations of Irish Traveller families in various media formats from audio to visual.

Dr Paul Delaney is a lecturer in the School of English, Trinity College, Dublin. He has contributed articles and reviews on various aspects of Irish literature to academic journals and books, and he is also the editor of Daniel Corkery's short fiction. He is currently completing a study of the history of representations of Travellers in Irish writing.

Dr Sinéad Ní Shúinéar, holds a Master's Degree from Jagiellonian University, Krakow, on Irish Traveller ethnicity and a PhD from University of Greenwich, London, on the Irish Traveller ethnolects, marriage patterns, and conflict. She held an Irish Research Council for the Humanities and Social Sciences post-doctoral fellowship and conducted research on Irish Traveller family trees and family histories. She has published many articles on Irish Travellers and Gypsies in Ireland in the Encyclopaedia of Ireland and in a number of anthologies.

Michael McDonagh is currently the General Manager of Navan Travellers Wordshops, a community based organisation in Co. Meath.

Dr Alice Binchy works with refugees, asylum seekers and migrants in West Tallaght Resource Centre, Dublin 24, where she is coordinator of Tallaght Intercultural Action's Education Project. She studied at NIHE Dublin (now Dublin City University) where she obtained BA and MA degrees in Communications, and at the University of Oxford where she was awarded a DPhil for her thesis on Shelta. She has various publications on Shelta. She is the co-author with Robbie McVeigh of *Travellers, Refugees and Racism in Tallaght*, a report published by West Tallaght Resource Centre. She is co-chair of Southside Travellers Action Group (STAG).